T0090514

# THE

# *Message*

# BEHIND THE

# *Miracle*

KAREN MARIE WATNEY

WESTBOW
PRESS®
A DIVISION OF THOMAS NELSON
& ZONDERVAN

WestBow Press books may be ordered through booksellers or by contacting:

WestBow Press
A Division of Thomas Nelson & Zondervan
1663 Liberty Drive
Bloomington, IN 47403
www.westbowpress.com
844-714-3454

New King James Version (NKJV)
Scripture taken from the New King James Version®. Copyright © 1982 by Thomas Nelson. Used by permission. All rights reserved.

ISBN: 979-8-3850-1842-0 (sc)
ISBN: 979-8-3850-1843-7 (e)

Library of Congress Control Number: 2024902387

Print information available on the last page.

WestBow Press rev. date: 02/08/2024

*Dear Reader,*

*I loved learning about the miracles of Jesus! I rejoiced each time a life was changed for the better! I wondered what it would have been like to watch Jesus heal someone. Just sensing His compassion made me love Him more. Each story is based on the Word of God. Then I added details and my own imagination.*

*Jesus is the most wonderful Man who has ever lived! We get to know Him better when we notice how He cared for every person and met their needs. His ministry was personal each time. He always focused on the one in front of Him.*

*Read through the Scripture verses for each story. Be familiar with what the Word says. Then read on and watch Jesus perform a miracle! Enjoy!*

*Blessings,*
*Karen*

# CONTENTS

# WATER INTO WINE AT CANA

## John 2:1-11

*John 2:1-4 On the third day there was a wedding in Cana of Galilee, and the mother of Jesus was there. Now both Jesus and His disciples were invited to the wedding. And when they ran out of wine, the mother of Jesus said to Him, "They have no wine." Jesus said to her, "Woman, what does your concern have to do with Me? My hour has not yet come."*

Cana of Galilee was located about 8 miles northeast of Nazareth (where Jesus and His family lived). It's quite possible that Mary was helping with wedding preparations for someone she was related to.

Weddings in those days lasted several days. Cana was a small village, so in that case, everyone who lived there would be invited. The occasion was very festive with music and dancing, good food and fellowship and good wine. The groom's family was responsible financially for pulling it off. To run out of anything would be embarrassing, but to run out of wine would have been the worst thing to happen! The wedding couple would likely be the laughing stock of the community. Running out of wine was a big deal! Mary was aware of the social ramifications.

## *Selah . . . Pause and Reflect*

*Mary knew Jesus not only had a caring heart; she had seen Him help her in many situations, being the oldest son of a widow. Mary wasn't telling Jesus what to do, she was simply giving the problem over to Him. Her mind was on the current problem.*

*<u>Heart Check:</u> The title "woman" does not mean a lack of respect. It was used in addressing people of rank. Jesus loved and honored His mother.*

*Jesus said to Mary, "What does your concern about wine have to do with Me?" In other words, "If you want Me to do a miracle, I'm not sure this is the right time. Things would not change for her if people saw the power of God manifest. But for Me it would be a big change! People would be coming to Me for some kind of blessing."*

*Jesus said, "My hour has not yet come." Those exact same words are in the following verses: John 7:6,8,30 and John 8:20. In all of these verses "His hour" referred to "His cross." <u>He</u> had to experience the cross before <u>we</u> could receive the new birth, which would eventually lead us to The Marriage Supper of the Lamb. (Revelation 19:9). Could the wine represent the joyful occasion of the Marriage Supper when Christ will have His bride, the church?*

\* \* \* \* \* \* \*

Mary told the servants, "Whatever He says to you, do it." When we face a difficulty, we would be wise to ask Jesus for a word to guide us. He knows everything about our circumstances. His Word may call for an action on our part, like it did for the servers.

## Selah . . . Pause and Reflect

*Instead of trying to figure out how we can solve our own problems, let's ask Jesus if there is something He wants us to know or to do. It may be a verse we can stand on. Many times He speaks something from the Scriptures.*

*Heart Check: Mary went to Jesus and gave Him the problem. Then she waited to see what He would say or do. We can do the same. We can wait quietly before Him in a listening mode. When He tells us something, let's make a practice of instantly obeying! In this story, Mary did the asking, the servants did the obeying.*

\* \* \* \* \* \* \*

There were six large stone water pots containing twenty or thirty gallons each. Jesus told the servants to fill them up with water. They filled them to the brim. Then Jesus said, "Draw some out now, and take it to the Master of the Feast." And they took it.

Six stone water pots would equal 120 to 150 gallons of wine when they were full. That is a very lot of wine! Even though the wedding festivities could last many days, there would still be plenty of wine left over. Did Jesus do that on purpose? Of course, He did! The wine left over would be a nice present for the bride and groom. They could sell some of the wine to help them get started in their married life. They could keep some for themselves. Jesus was generous! A king could be generous, right? King Jesus gave the best wedding gift ever! Every time that young couple had a glass of wine with their dinner, they thought of their beautiful, joyful wedding, where the King of kings showed up to bless them!

## Selah . . . Pause and Reflect

*These servants knew how to serve! They didn't make decisions on their own, like only filling the pots half full or even less. They filled them to the brim. Maybe they each had a two-gallon pitcher to use, so that would have taken them some time to finish! They simply obeyed, not slowing down until the job was completed. Notice that they didn't make comments. They didn't say, "What good is water? They want wine!" No mocking or complaining, just simple obedience.*

*<u>Heart Check:</u> When Jesus told the servants to draw some out and take it to the master of the feast, they didn't whisper to each other, "Boy, this is dumb!" They just obeyed. When did the miracle take place? Was it before Jesus told the servants to draw some out? Was it while the servants walked to where the Master of the Feast was? Was it when he took a drink?*

*Those humble and obedient servants went home that night with A Story To Tell!! THEY were part of a miracle! Water was turned into wine; something that had never happened before! They told everyone they knew that a Man named Jesus made that miracle happen! How exciting! They would never forget that night! They would never forget Jesus!*

\* \* \* \* \* \* \*

The Master of the Feast was very impressed by the excellent quality of the wine! He called over the bridegroom and complimented him on such fine wine. The Master said, "Every man at the beginning sets out the good wine, and when the guests have well drunk, then the inferior. You have kept the good wine until now!"

## Selah . . . Pause and Reflect

*Jesus knew how to turn an unfortunate situation into a wonderful occasion! The wedding party faced embarrassment and were especially grateful for their problem to be solved! Their good reputation in the community was maintained, thanks to Jesus.*

*Notice the humility of Jesus. He quietly came back to the party once the wine was made. The majority of the people there had no idea that a miracle had just taken place. He entered into conversation with others, as if nothing important had just happened. As the night wore on, the whispers went around until eventually everyone knew what Jesus did.*

*Heart Check: For Seniors reading this, Take the words of the Master of the Feast and apply them to yourself: Jesus has kept the good part of your life until now! Say, "Jesus, we will serve You in our latter years with Joy in our hearts. We know that You can take our ordinary lives and turn them into something extra-ordinary! We love You, Jesus. We trust You, Jesus."*

\* \* \* \* \* \*

This is the beginning of the Miracle Signs that Jesus did. Each one revealed His Glory. (John 2:11). The disciples saw a new side of Jesus and their level of faith in Him increased. They most likely shared this miracle with anybody who would listen! They were observing Jesus and learning Who this Man was. They were impressed!

Future healings and deliverances were called Signs and Wonders. During three years of ministry, Jesus performed countless Signs and Wonders!

The "Glory" of God rested upon Jesus in the form of "Power" to perform miracles. Everyone knew that only God had the power to do miracles! Jesus must be the Messiah, the Son of God! "Glory" and "Power" go together.

## Selah . . . Pause and Reflect

*Wine comes from grapes, not water! For Jesus to get wine from water is definitely a miracle! Only God can do miracles. Jesus was a Man whose power came from God. Jesus depended on the Father to tell Him what to do. When He simply obeyed, the power of God flowed through Him.*

*Heart Check: Jesus led His disciples in taking communion in Matthew 26:26-28. The bread and the wine are symbols to remind all of us of the sacrifice Jesus made. Jesus paid the price so we could be free from sin and its consequences, such as sickness. We are now rightly related to our Father God, like Adam and Eve were. The Blood of Jesus is the most powerful thing in the whole universe!*

\* \* \* \* \* \* \*

### WHO IS JESUS FOR US TODAY?

*Jesus began His ministry by bringing forth WINE, a symbol for BLOOD. The last and greatest thing He did was the shedding of His BLOOD, setting mankind free from the slavery of sin.*

\* \* \* \* \* \* \*

*WHAT DID WE LEARN FROM THIS STORY?*

*Cana was a small village. The first miracle Jesus performed was not in a large, important place.*

*Jesus was <u>invited</u> to the wedding. Mary <u>invited</u> Him to help. He wants us to <u>invite</u> Him into every part of our lives.*

*The servants were amazing! They did exactly what they were told and were respectful. They were rewarded with the knowledge that they had participated in a MIRACLE!*

*Let's be like the servants: Listen and Obey!*

*Jesus performed miracles because, from His baptism the Spirit lived in Him, and He was an obedient Son.*

# THE NOBLEMAN'S SON

John 4:46-54

*John 4:46-47 And So Jesus came again to Cana of Galilee where He had made the water into wine. And there was a certain nobleman whose son was sick at Capernaum. When he heard that Jesus had come out of Judea into Galilee, He went to Him and implored Him to come down and heal his son, for he was at the point of death.*

Jesus came from having a conversation with Nicodemus in Jerusalem (John 3), and then another conversation with the woman at the well in Samaria. (John 4:1-42). He is now in Cana, which is part of the area of Galilee where He is from. The village of Cana was located between Nazareth and Capernaum. This area was very familiar to Jesus and some people would have known Him and His family as He grew up.

The nobleman was a royal official who worked in the court of Herod Antipas in Capernaum. He was a Gentile who had become aware of the miracles of Jesus. Perhaps he knew someone who had seen Jesus heal people during the recent Passover Festival in Jerusalem.

Now, this nobleman desperately needed a miracle! His son was very sick, even thought to be close to dying. This is a desperate dad! As soon as he learned Jesus was nearby, he set out to walk the twenty miles from Capernaum to Cana to find Him.

## Selah . . . Pause and Reflect

*John 4:45 tell us that when Jesus came to Galilee, the Galileans received Him, having seen all the things He did in Jerusalem at the feast, for they also had gone to the feast. In those days, news of amazing healings traveled fast from one community to another! They didn't have our modern ways to communicate, like phones and the internet. They had each other! Theirs was a very relational culture.*

*<u>Heart Check:</u> The nobleman would not have known to seek Jesus out unless someone told him about the miracles they saw. Do we need to take a lesson from their culture? Do we get together and talk about the things of the Lord? Do we pray for people "in person" showing our care for them? Do we make friends with our neighbors who don't know Jesus?*

\* \* \* \* \* \*

This desperate dad begged Jesus to come to heal his son. "You must come," he thought, "You are my only hope right now!" Jesus said, "*Unless you people see signs and wonders, you will by no means believe.*" This response from Jesus must have surprised the man, but it did not deter him! He did not give up! He continued to plead with Jesus to come and heal his boy before he died!

## Selah . . . Pause and Reflect

*Jesus said, "Unless you people." The "you" is plural, which means He was including the crowd that had gathered to see what Jesus would do. Jesus knew that in every crowd there were serious seekers who would end up giving their lives to Him and be determined to follow Him with all their heart.*

*There were also people who just wanted to see a miracle and then go on their way, having no desire for a relationship with The Healer Himself. There were the curious onlookers at the edges of the crowd, simply checking out this traveling preacher, perhaps even looking for something they could fault Him for.*

*Heart Check: Miracles performed in Jesus' day, and in our day, are meant to point people to faith in Jesus as Savior. (John 6:26-29,40).*

\* \* \* \* \* \* \*

The nobleman heard about the amazing compassion of Jesus. He was told that even the most difficult healings were easy for Jesus. That compassion, and the power behind it, were foremost in his mind when he urged Jesus to come immediately! Now, being in His presence, standing in front of Him, he could sense welcoming warmth coming from Jesus, even without His words.

## Selah . . . Pause and Reflect

*People give off signs of their real self when we are near them. We can tell if someone is impatient, tired or happy just by observation! What did they see when they spent time with Jesus? They saw someone who was peaceful, not one bit rattled by any difficult situation. They saw kindness personified. They knew each person Jesus talked to was important to Him. They noticed the deep-down joy in Him, even when He was tired. They "felt" His love, not any condemnation. Everyone knew He cared deeply just for them!*

*Heart Check: How do we see Jesus when we talk to Him? Do we think that He is looking at all the things we don't like about ourselves? Do we wonder if He really cares about our situation? Maybe He is too busy taking care of other people who deserve His presence more. All of those kind of thoughts are from the enemy - kick them out! Visualize (meditate on) the real Jesus!*

\* \* \* \* \* \* \*

The nobleman was hanging on to his belief that Jesus could and would save his son from death. He believed that Jesus had to be present to perform a miracle. After urging Jesus to come to Capernaum the second time, he heard Jesus say, "Go your way, your son lives." He believed the Words that Jesus spoke to him and he left to go back to his home. "Evidently, Jesus chose a different way of answering my plea for help," he thought. "He doesn't have to be right near my son after all. That's fine with me. I believe what He said, Your son WILL live!"

## Selah . . . Pause and Reflect

*This is a picture of how faith works! There is no arguing about it, no "show me a sign" and then I'll have faith. Those Words settled in his heart that Jesus answered his request. He chose to not care about the "how" Jesus did it! He was simply grateful that He "would" do it.*

*Heart Check: Do we feel it is important that we tell Jesus "how" to answer our prayer? Is it okay for Him to decide the best way?*

\* \* \* \* \* \* \*

As the nobleman walked back those twenty miles to Capernaum, he had peace. Along the way he was greeted by his servants who met him and said, "Your son lives!" How awesome to hear that news, but then again, he knew in his heart already that was the case. He asked the servants about the time the boy "got better." They told him the seventh hour, which was exactly when Jesus said, *Go your way, your son lives.*

## *Selah . . . Pause and Reflect*

*The man thought there would be a recovery time. The boy was made completely well all of a sudden! Jesus blessed this man in a way he wasn't expecting! Our Savior gives us more than we ask!*

*Heart Check: Lord Jesus, Your blessings always make us rich! Your Words are Powerful! We can rest in what You say in Your Word, the Bible. Just like the Nobleman, we will go our way, knowing You will fulfill Your Word for us.*

\* \* \* \* \* \* \*

### *WHO IS JESUS FOR US TODAY?*

*Jesus is our WAY MAKER! He is Lord over sickness and death!*

*He makes a way when there seems to be no way.*

\* \* \* \* \* \* \*

### *WHAT DID WE LEARN FROM THIS STORY?*

*It was a crisis in his life that brought
the nobleman to Jesus.*

*Sometimes our faith is tested. Jesus is all about helping us build our faith in His ability and His willingness.*

*Corrections can be viewed as stepping stones or stumbling blocks to our faith. The nobleman used Jesus' gentle rebuke as a stepping stone and kept his faith strong. He did not become offended!*

*Jesus reacted to the nobleman's faith with a simple promise - "Go your way; your son lives."*

*Jesus did not have to be present for the son to be healed. We can be confident that He answers our long-distance prayers.*

*The whole family could rejoice that they got to see this precious boy grow up!*

# MAN WITH UNCLEAN SPIRIT

## Mark 1:21-28     Luke 4:31-37

*Luke 4:31-32 Then He went down to Capernaum, a city of Galilee, and was teaching them on the Sabbaths. And they were astonished at His teaching, for His word was with authority.*

Following His rejection in Nazareth, Jesus and His disciples moved on to the city of Capernaum. Each Sabbath Jesus would teach the people at their synagogue. He was warmly welcomed by this community. They listened carefully and said that He spoke with such authority. His teaching was so different from the religious scholars.

## Selah . . . Pause and Reflect

*Picture yourself eagerly coming to the synagogue each Sabbath to get a chance to hear this new Teacher! Perhaps you hurried and arrived early to get a good seat, now that so many new people came. There was something electric about the powerful truths that this Man brought! You could sense the Life in everything He said and you hung on His every Word!*

*Heart Check: Does it matter if we read our Bible consistently? Does it matter that we focus on the Words of Jesus? Our Savior spoke with such insight and anointing. Do we desire His Words to dramatically penetrate our hearts and change us? Let's say the same as those who were in the synagogue: "We are astonished at His teaching, for His Word is with authority."*

\* \* \* \* \* \* \*

In the congregation that day there was a man who had a spirit of an unclean demon. He cried out with a loud voice saying, "Go away and leave us alone! I know Who You are, the Holy One of God. Did You come to destroy us?"

## Selah . . . Pause and Reflect

*There are two kingdoms operating in our world: The Kingdom of God and the Kingdom of Satan. This man's spirit was a part of the Kingdom of Satan. The ways of Satan's kingdom are evil and involve tormenting people. The Kingdom of God has come to set people free from torment!*

*This spirit may have been lying dormant for some time. It was the presence of Jesus that drew it out. Apparently, demons know their end will come some day at the hands of the superior power of the Creator God. Jesus took Satan's authority over mankind away when He rose from the dead. (Revelation 1:18). Now, Jesus holds ALL authority over death and the unseen realm. He always brings freedom and release from evil domination. Living in torment is not His way.*

*Heart Check: The unclean spirit called Jesus the "Holy One of God." This is interesting, since Jesus was just recently rejected in Nazareth. Read Luke 4:28-34 to see the contrast. The leaders of the synagogue in Nazareth were ready to throw Jesus off a cliff! A demon spirit in Capernaum was calling Him the Holy One! Some men don't know who Jesus is, while demons are in awe and fear of Him!*

\* \* \* \* \* \* \*

15

Jesus rebuked the spirit saying, "Be quiet, and come out of him!" When the demon had cried out with a loud voice, convulsed him and thrown him down in their midst, it came out of him and did not hurt him.

Jesus was doing in this synagogue the same thing He did later in the temple. (John 2:13-16). He was casting out what did not belong there! Only what reflects God should be in a place of worship, a holy place.

## Selah . . . Pause and Reflect

*Jesus told the demon to be quiet! He would not allow a demon to have a voice. Let's do the same! We have one Shepherd and we hear His voice! (John 10:27). We won't hear the voice of the "accuser." He wants us to agree with his accusations and feel bad about ourselves. Not happening!*

*Heart Check: We don't have to tolerate evil thoughts or influences. Jesus lives inside of us and He is Lord of All! 1 John 4:4 tells us, "He who is in you is greater than he who is in the world." Reject all thoughts that don't line up with the Word of God, the Love of God and the Character of God.*

\* \* \* \* \* \* \*

The people were amazed and said among themselves, "What kind of a man is this who has such power and authority? He commands demons to come out and they obey Him!" It is interesting that the demon knew who Jesus was before the people did! This miracle was told until everyone in the surrounding region knew about it! Good news about Jesus traveled fast!

## Selah . . . Pause and Reflect

Jesus had authority in <u>what He said</u> in His teaching (Mark 1:22) and <u>what He did</u> in His ministry of healing and deliverance. (Mark 1:27). This pattern is also seen in the early church when we read accounts in the book of Acts. The authority of the Word is <u>God speaking</u>. The authority that brings life-changing actions is <u>God doing</u>.

<u>Heart Check:</u> What we say is important! Our words reflect what we believe in our heart. Jesus won the battle on the cross for us. He defeated all evil principalities and powers. (Colossians 2:15 and Luke 10:19). Since He lives in us, that means we don't have to be defeated. We can tell our neighbors they don't have to be defeated either!

\* \* \* \* \* \*

WHO IS JESUS FOR US TODAY?
Jesus has AUTHORITY! He is our Champion who rescues us!

He sets us free from Satan's influence and power!

\* \* \* \* \* \*

WHAT DID WE LEARN FROM THIS STORY?

We are eager to hear a Word from Jesus because everything He says will benefit us!

Jesus spoke of what was truth from the Father's perspective. He heard God in prayer.

*We can rely on His authority over all the works of the enemy, which includes sickness.*

*Jesus loves it when WE, not demons, proclaim Who He is, The Holy One of God.*

# PETER'S MOTHER-IN-LAW

Mathew 8:14-15     Mark 1:29-31     Luke 4:38-39

*Mark 1:29-30 Now as soon as they had come out of the synagogue, they entered the house of Simon and Andrew, with James and John. But Simon's wife's mother lay sick with a fever, and they told Him about her at once.*

*Luke 4:38 Now He arose from the synagogue and entered Simon's house. But Simon's wife's mother was sick with a high fever and they made request of Him concerning her.*

The healing of Peter's wife's mother was one of the first demonstrations of the healing power of Jesus. Three gospel writers felt this story was important and each one put a brief explanation of what happened. Matthew simply recorded: *Now when Jesus had come into Peter's house, He saw his wife's mother lying sick with a fever.* Luke tells us that the fever was "high." Mark added that Simon and Andrew lived in that house and he mentioned that James and John were invited there, along with Jesus.

## Selah . . . Pause and Reflect

*Peter's mother-in-law didn't have anything to do with her healing! It was Peter and the others that asked Jesus to heal her. Jesus works through families. When one member of a family encounters Jesus, it is not long before others follow. This is the beautiful thing about being related to one another; we can learn and grow and change simply because we share life together.*

*Heart Check: Can a person get healed when we pray for them, even though they are not praying or believing for themselves to be healed? This story would suggest that we can pray and expect to see God answer! We are already connected to our families, so it is natural that we care about them and will pray in faith for them, whether they know the Lord or not.*

\* \* \* \* \* \*

According to Matthew, Jesus touched her hand. Mark says He gently took her by the hand and lifted her up. Luke writes that Jesus stood over her and rebuked the fever. He did all of these things for her! Touching, lifting up by the hand and rebuking were all things Jesus did in His healing ministry. Suddenly, she had energy and vitality! She soon was in the kitchen getting lunch ready for everyone!

## Selah . . . Pause and Reflect

*Think about how this woman would feel with a high fever. Her whole body ached, she was weak, headache, chills. The whole ordeal was so not fun! Then, all of a sudden the most amazing thing happened! Jesus was there and everything dramatically changed! Once He rebuked the fever and helped her sit up, all of those symptoms completely left her!*

*Heart Check: Families are important to us! It's the place where we "belong." If a family member struggles with a health issue, we can pray for them. When we believe God's Word and speak it out, it is as if Jesus is praying for them through us. He lives inside of us and the Father answers our prayers the same as when Jesus prays.*

\* \* \* \* \* \* \*

*WHO IS JESUS FOR US TODAY?*

*Jesus LOVES FAMILIES! We are all IMPORTANT to Him.*

*He wants to heal you and your family members!*

\* \* \* \* \* \*

*WHAT DID WE LEARN FROM THIS STORY?*

*We can expect God to heal someone simply because we pray.
They don't have to go to Jesus themselves first.*

*We have authority to pray for healing because of the Name
of Jesus and because of His Blood shed for us.*

*Jesus demonstrated some ways to pray for the sick. We can touch
the person. We can take the person by the hand and help them
get up. We can also rebuke the symptoms.*

*Jesus did not hesitate to pray for Peter's mother-in-law. We
won't hesitate as well; we care for family members.*

*Jesus knew that sickness was not part of the Creation plan.
He also knew that the curse of sin and sickness would
be broken by the stripes He would take.*

*The will of Jesus regarding healing is plain to see since He
healed multitudes of people! We can confidently follow
in His footsteps because of 1 John 5:14.*

# WILLING TO HEAL A LEPER

Mathew 8:1-4          Mark 1:40-45          Luke 5:12-15

*Matthew 8:2 And behold, a leper came and worshiped Him, saying, "Lord, if You are willing, You can make me clean."*

Doctor Luke tells us this man was "full of leprosy." (Luke 5:12). That meant that his whole body was affected by this terrible disease and also possibly that he was in the advanced stage.

The man heard that Messiah was coming to his town! With a mixture of a lot of hope and some desperation, he was determined to make his way to the road where a crowd had gathered to see Jesus. As he hurried along, he cried out, "unclean, unclean," as he was required to do. People scattered quickly to avoid touching him and becoming contaminated. Soon he saw Jesus just up ahead.

## Selah . . . Pause and Reflect

*Since the disease was highly contagious, lepers were forced to live by themselves, away from their families and friends. (Leviticus 13:46). For him to come into a public area and defy the "rules for a leper" was a courageous thing for him to do. He was willing to risk going against the regulations of Jewish society to possibly get his miracle.*

*Heart Check: Do we tend to give up hope for a miracle when the person we are praying for is in the advanced stage of their illness? Is our faith weakened by what we can see in the natural? This man ignored the fears and doubts that were shouting loudly in his mind. He purposefully chose to go with his heart and believe that if Jesus was the Messiah, then there was nothing impossible for Him to do!*

* * * * * * *

The leper saw Jesus in the crowd, and he shuffled as fast as he could, moving toward Him. Where he had his focus was critical. He had to look away from his pain, the open sores and putrid smell. He looked away from unanswered prayers and discouragement. He set those things aside. Ever since he heard from others that compassion and power flowed through this Man Jesus, he gained hope. He tried not to think about his own unworthiness as an unclean person.

He was told that, as a leper, God was punishing him for his sin. He could not remember anything he did to go against the Laws of God. It didn't help his self-esteem any to realize people looked at him in such a negative way.

When the leper reached Jesus, he dropped to his knees. His body language showed his heart of humility and his worship of Jesus. He called Him Lord. He said, "Lord, if You are willing, You can make me clean." ("Would You take delight in healing me?") That was the question that lingered in his mind.

## Selah . . . Pause and Reflect

*Has anyone ever told you that you were "not good enough?" We have an enemy, the accuser, that whispers lies in our head - we will never measure up, never be good enough. Jesus whispers just the opposite, that we are precious in His sight.*

*He loves us with an everlasting love (Jeremiah 31:3) and He has a wonderful future planned for us! (Jeremiah 29:11).*

*What an awesome way the man came to Jesus - humbly, on his knees. That speaks volumes about his attitude. He was the lesser, Jesus was the greater. He was dependent, Jesus was in charge. He was simply a man, Jesus was the God-Man.*

*<u>Heart Check:</u> We can tell the level of our faith by what we think and what comes out of our mouth. Our faith grows when we spend time meditating on God's promises in the Bible. Let's put our name in each one! We can be convinced in our heart that God is good and that He will honor His Word.*

*God doesn't want us analyzing ourselves to see if we are worthy of His favor and blessings. He wants us to take our eyes off from ourselves and simply accept what the Word says. God put us in Christ when we were born again. Being found in Him makes us worthy. We can focus on Jesus our Healer.*

\* \* \* \* \* \* \*

Then Jesus, moved with compassion, stretched out His hand and touched the leper. It is significant that Jesus touched this man *before* He healed him. The touch of Jesus spoke loud and clear to this man's heart! It didn't matter if others rejected him, Jesus did not! He is the only One that really matters! The man was still leprous, Jesus didn't care. He gave him the touch of friendship and acceptance. Jesus didn't contract leprosy from him, which was presumed by most. Instead, the healing virtue of Jesus went to the leper and made him thoroughly cleansed!

## Selah . . . Pause and Reflect

*This man was questioning the willingness of Jesus to heal someone such as himself. He had experienced rejection so long that it made him feel quite unworthy of anything good, especially from God.*

*Do you think that the touch of Jesus meant something special to the leper, deeply affecting him? Jesus wants to touch us in the same way. He does it through loving, affirming words, whispered to our soul when we are praying or reading our Bible.*

*Heart Check: Do negative thoughts rule over us? Can we have the same boldness this man had in coming to Jesus? Ephesians 3:11-12 says that because we are in Christ, we can come boldly to the Lord and He will welcome us! It doesn't say we have to be perfect first!*

\* \* \* \* \* \*

Jesus said to him, "I am willing, be cleansed." As soon as He had spoken; immediately the leprosy began to leave him, and he was cleansed!

All at once the leper got to experience the amazing, compassionate heart of Jesus. It just took five words: "I am willing, be cleansed!" Five words, and the power behind those words changed the man's whole situation and his future! What extravagant thankfulness and joy sprang from his heart toward his Lord as he watched his skin turn back to being normal! He could hardly wait to see his family, to be a part of his community again and to worship with more enthusiasm than anyone else at the synagogue!

## *Selah . . . Pause and Reflect*

*Those words uttered by Jesus: "I am willing," are absolutely life changing if you choose to believe that he is saying that to you as well. Jesus is the same yesterday, today and forever. (Hebrews 13:8). Do you believe Jesus is saying that to you? Hear Him say this to you: "Whatever your issue is, I am here to help you, I am willing, dear one."*

*We've already looked at the fact that Jesus was "moved with compassion" when He interacted with the leper. Jesus knew him through and through by the Spirit. He knew all about his past and present pain, both physical and emotional. Jesus could also perceive the leper's determined faith (even though he had a question about the willingness of Jesus). Our honest questions don't disqualify us when we bring them to Jesus. He wants us to be real with Him.*

*<u>Heart Check:</u> Compassion is the strong emotion of Huge Love that comes from the soul of Jesus. Jesus has that same level of deep compassion toward each one of us today. That is hard to picture, since we know ourselves so well! Think about it. If He did not have that deep, deep compassion for us, why would He allow Himself to go through the horrors of the scourging and the cross? He did it all for us - to set us free, just like He set the leper free. It was because of His amazing love for us that He endured the agony. In His eyes, we were worth it!*

\* \* \* \* \* \*

## WHO IS JESUS FOR US TODAY?

*Jesus is ALWAYS WILLING to heal anyone who needs a healing.*

*He will not turn anyone away who comes to Him.*

\* \* \* \* \* \*

## WHAT DID WE LEARN FROM THIS STORY?

*Refuse discouragement if the situation gets worse! Press forward with a focus on Jesus only, not the symptoms.*

*Don't dwell on thoughts of rejection. Lay all of it at the feet of Jesus. He brings freedom and heart healing.*

*Hope and faith pushed the leper to have courage to come to Jesus in the crowd. Don't give up!*

*The Lord, through His Word, will give us our true identity. We do not accept negative labels, like "unclean, unworthy."*

*The first thing the leper did was to worship! That humble attitude is pleasing to God.*

# PARALYTIC LET DOWN THROUGH THE ROOF

### Matthew 9:1-8    Mark 2:1-12    Luke 5:17-26

*Mark 2:1-2 And again He entered Capernaum after some days, and it was heard that He was in the house. Immediately many gathered together, so that there was no longer room to receive them, not even near the door. And He preached the Word to them.*

*Luke 5:17 Now it happened on a certain day as He was teaching, that there were Pharisees and teachers of the law sitting by, who had come out of every town of Galilee, Judea and Jerusalem. And the power of the Lord was present to heal.*

This event happened early in the ministry of Jesus, before He named all of His twelve disciples. Simon Peter, Andrew, James and John were with Him. (Luke 5:1-11). Shortly following this miracle, Jesus went on to call Matthew while he was sitting at his tax booth. (Matthew 9:9).

When word went out that Jesus was in the area, a crowd quickly gathered, eager to hear Him teach and perhaps to see a miracle. We're told that a number of Pharisees and teachers of the Law also came to learn from the wisdom of Jesus. NOT! They were there to find something to accuse Him of! Already Jesus had a reputation for being a Sabbath-breaker. They were convinced that He was a false prophet. They were determined to protect their people from His lies.

## Selah . . . Pause and Reflect

*Luke 5:17 tells us that "the power of the Lord was present to heal." Wow! What an amazing and gracious God we have! Those very Pharisees could have been blessed with healing in their bodies that day! All they had to do was step aside from the strict Sabbath rules that men made and just follow the ways of God! His ways are kind, loving and beneficial to people. The ways of the Pharisees and teachers of the Law tended to restrict people.*

*<u>Heart Check:</u> What does the Word say about who Jesus is? Even as children, we can get ideas that are contrary to what the Bible says. Do we picture God with a big stick ready to hit us when we don't behave? Or, do we picture Him coming alongside us, helping us? The Father put all of His wrath for sin on Jesus at the cross, so He has no wrath lefts to give to us! He's not mad at us!! He loves each one of us with big loves!*

\* \* \* \* \* \* \*

*There are differing accounts of how the men opened a hole in the roof to let their friend down near Jesus. The following paragraph shows one possibility. Each reader can picture their own method of accomplishing the task of lowering this man and his mat down to Jesus. The point is not about the "how" they lowered him, but about how much "faith and determination" they showed in their quest for this crippled man's healing. Back to the story...*

They saw that the home was crowded with people, so they climbed the outside stairs to the flat roof and removed some of the tiling, making an opening. Carefully, they let their friend and his mat down right in front of Jesus. That bold action must have surprised everyone in the room!

## Selah . . . Pause and Reflect

*Perhaps the man himself heard stories of Jesus healing people. Did he ask his friends to assist him in his quest for healing? Or, could it have been the four men who heard of the miracle-working Man of God?*

*It's obvious those men were determined to see a miracle for their friend, even to the point of being desperate! Did they wonder if Jesus would be gone tomorrow and they would miss their chance? Making a hole in someone's roof is not the normal way to enter a home! (Maybe they came back later and fixed the roof!)*

*Heart Check: These men knew if they could get to Jesus, their friend would be healed. How did they know that? They heard healing stories from the ministry of Jesus. These stories, both Biblical ones and current ones, are meant to encourage us to believe in Jesus as our Healer too!*

* * * * * * *

When Jesus saw their faith, He said to the paralytic, "Son, your sins are forgiven you."

## Selah . . . Pause and Reflect

*Let's take note of the phrase, "When Jesus saw their faith," in this sentence. The word "their" indicates Jesus is perceiving the faith of the four men and probably including the paralyzed man's faith as well. Jesus knew in His Spirit that these men, all five of them, CAME EXPECTING!*

*As we have seen from other healing stories, faith is very important to Jesus. These men were eager to receive a miracle from Jesus! Their hearts and minds were set. "Our friend is getting healed today by Jesus! We will do what it takes to make that happen." Real faith is supported by love. (Galatians 5:6). These four men loved their paralytic friend.*

*After Jesus saw their faith, He went on to speak to the paralyzed man. He said, "Son, your sins are forgiven you." We don't know the reasons behind why Jesus would have said that to him. We do know that Jesus received words from the Father in each situation He encountered. (John 5:30). It's possible the man was feeling shame over something he did years earlier. If that was the case, for Jesus to assure him of complete forgiveness would have been very meaningful to him. No more guilt feelings nagging at him.*

*Perhaps the main reason Jesus said, "Your sins are forgiven" was to address the issue of His Lordship over sin and the evil that caused it. God is opposed to evil in every way. Before evil infected the Garden of Eden, there was no sin and no sickness. The goal of God is to bring complete wholeness to people: spirit, soul and body. 1 John 3:8 says, "For this purpose the Son of God was manifested, that He might destroy the works of the devil."*

*Heart Check: When people came to Jesus for healing, He did not ask them to confess their sins first. There would be a time when Jesus would hang on the cross, to pay for all the sin of all mankind, so we could all be forgiven. That is an amazing accomplishment, something which none of us will ever deserve, all grace.*

*For us, ones who know the Lord, keeping a short account of wrong thinking and wrong doing is wisdom because we reap what we sow. The Bible says, if we are forgiven, we must forgive others. Matthew 18:21-35 is where Jesus makes this whole subject very clear.*

\* \* \* \* \* \* \*

The scribes and Pharisees began to reason in their hearts - "Who is this who speaks blasphemies? Who can forgive sins but God alone?" A person to claim they were God or the Son or God, and they were merely human, would be charged with blasphemy. It was the charge of blasphemy that led to the crucifixion of Jesus. (Matthew 26:63-66).

Jesus perceived that they had such reasoning. He asked them, "Why do you reason about these things in your hearts? Which is easier to say to the paralytic, 'Your sins are forgiven you,' or to say, 'Arise, take up your bed and walk?'"

## Selah . . . Pause and Reflect

*Jesus wanted everyone to know that He had authority on earth to forgive sins. This was a blatant way to say that He was part of the Godhead, the promised Messiah. The religious bunch just could not buy that! They firmly held the belief that He was a Sabbath breaker, punishable by death. In reality, Jesus did not break any of the Laws of Moses that God gave. He kept them all. (Mark 2:23-28). He was breaking the petty rules put upon people by religious leaders. The Sabbath was meant to be a lovely day of rest to enjoy the presence of the Lord and be refreshed. Now, if they picked up their mat, it would be considered "work," and they would be reprimanded!*

*Heart Check: Jesus was prepared to give the Pharisees and scribes a challenge. He wanted them to think through the "if this, then that" point of view. "If" Jesus was a man empowered by Jehovah God and He could make a paralyzed person completely well and whole, "Then" that same One had the authority from God to forgive sins. He proceeded to prove His ability to heal a completely helpless man. Soooo, that proved His authority, as God's Son, to forgive sin.*

\* \* \* \* \* \*

"But that you may know that the Son of Man has power on earth to forgive sins" - He said to the man who was paralyzed, "I say to you arise, take up your bed, and go to your house." Immediately, he rose up before them, took up what he had been lying on, and departed to his own house, glorifying God. The people were all amazed, and shouted praises to God!

## Selah . . . Pause and Reflect

*The charge of blasphemy would have been correct if Jesus had not been the Son of God. A blasphemy is a verbal affront to God's majesty and the penalty for such was death by stoning. (Leviticus 24:15-16). Jesus, as coming from God, was given delegated authority (power) to forgive sins.*

*Heart Check: Multitudes of people were healed by Jesus. We are not told details about them individually. This story about the paralytic is the fifth specific healing miracle Jesus performed out of the twenty six listed in the gospels. This happened in late A.D. 27 during the Galilean Ministry of Jesus. Jesus was crucified in A.D. 30.*

*The dividing line between those who loved Jesus and those who hated Him was drawn early in His ministry. Perhaps that was partly because of this occasion when Jesus claimed He could forgive sin as well as heal. We were already told there were Pharisees and teachers of the law sitting by, who had come out of every town of Galilee, Judea and Jerusalem to check out every word Jesus said. Obviously, they were not in agreement with His words about forgiving someone's sins. They could hardly wait to put to death this " false prophet."*

*Jesus attended the three feasts held in Jerusalem each year. That great city was home to a multitude of Scribes and Pharisees who thought Jesus was worthy of death. Jesus knew the timing of the cross and did not want to be arrested before the right time.*

*He only did a few miracles while He was in Jerusalem. For example, He only healed one man at the Pool of Bethesda where there were many in need of healing. (John 5:1-47). Jesus did not want huge crowds of people flocking to Him in Jerusalem, causing even more concern and hatred by the religious establishment.*

*Jesus healed in Capernaum and other cities in the Galilean Region, far north of Jerusalem. He was accepted and welcomed by many of those cities and towns.*

\* \* \* \* \* \* \*

*WHO IS JESUS FOR US TODAY?*

*Jesus FORGIVES and HEALS.*

*He meets the needs of expectant people.*

\* \* \* \* \* \* \*

*WHAT DID WE LEARN FROM THIS STORY?*

*These men brought a friend to Jesus! Their expression
of faith was public, seen by everyone.*

*Faith and determination go together! They were going
to see a miracle that day for their friend!*

*These men did not question the Lordship of Jesus. They knew
He had power to heal and they expected it.*

*Faith overcomes all obstacles when Love is involved. We
benefit by connecting with like-minded people.*

*Jesus wanted the religious crowd to recognize that He was
the Son of God. He had Godly authority to forgive sins.*

*This precious man got two blessings that day! Jesus said that
his sins were forgiven, AND he got to walk home! Yay!*

*Biblical stories and current testimonies of healing are meant to
encourage us to believe in Jesus as our Healer!*

# HEALED AT THE POOL
# OF BETHESDA

## John 5:2-12

*John 5:2-3 Now there is in Jerusalem by the Sheep Gate a pool, which is called in Hebrew Bethesda, having five porches. In these lay a great multitude of sick people, blind, lame, paralyzed, waiting for the moving of the water.*

Tradition is that an angel supernaturally stirred the waters in this pool. When that happened, God's healing grace was present. The first person to step into the pool would be healed. Whether it was an angel or an intermittent spring causing the bubbling of the waters, the first person in the pool was indeed set free from their infirmity! A miracle really did happen every time for that first one!

These occasional miracles were enough to give the rest of the crowd hope. "Maybe I will be the first one to get into the pool the next time," they thought. So they would stay and wait and hope.

*John 5:5 Now a certain man was there who had an infirmity thirty-eight years.* That's a really long time! Picture yourself sitting next to him for all those years. You also were lame. What would each day be like?

Why would Jesus look for only one man out of that multitude? Couldn't He just heal them all? There were many occasions when Jesus did heal every sick person that joined with a crowd and came to Him.

## Selah . . . Pause and Reflect

*In the same chapter, we find one possible answer to why Jesus sought only this one lame man. John 5:19 says, "Most assuredly, I say to you, the Son can do nothing of Himself, but what He sees the Father do; for whatever He does, the Son also does in like manner."*

*Jesus simply followed the instructions of His Father and He knew that the man had been in that crippled condition for 38 years. This helpless man kept waiting for the stirring of the waters. Year after year he wanted to be the first one in the pool, but that never happened.*

*<u>Heart check:</u> Jesus wanted him to see that his focus was misplaced. His healing wasn't to come because an angel stirred the waters. His hope must be in Jesus, the One greater than angels. Jesus was present to heal him!*

*Jesus also wanted to minister to the discouragement that had taken over the man's soul. The man had thought only on what was not happening. Jesus wanted him to look Godward to supernatural possibilities! What about us? Are we focused on the promises of God or on our condition? Moses encouraged Joshua to meditate in God's Word and he would prosper and have good success. (Joshua 1:8). Being made well is prospering!*

\* \* \* \* \* \* \*

Jesus said, "Do you want to be made well?" That seems a strange question to ask someone, but it's not. Answering this question will bring out the true mindset of a sick person. The man did not answer the question Jesus asked. Instead of giving Jesus a yes or no answer, he gave Jesus the excuse that no one would help him get into the pool! It was always someone else's fault that he didn't get healed. Did this man think of Jesus as possibly being his "helper" rather than his "Healer?"

## Selah . . . Pause and Reflect

*What are some excuses for not wanting to get well? "If I get out of this wheelchair, I will have to go out and try to find a job!" "I'm getting a nice check from the government now." "People pay attention to me; if I were well, they would ignore me." "Others are healed, but I'm not good enough."*

*The excuse he gave to Jesus was that he didn't have the help he needed. Did the people around him leave him behind? When that happens over and over, it's easy for self-pity and even resentment to set in.*

*Could it be that the thing the man needed was a "heart healing" that would allow him to forgive people? Bitterness is like a cancer that can color everything. Keeping an offense alive will only hurt ourselves.*

*Heart check: Jesus always wanted to bring people to a place of faith. This meant they had to have a determination to be healed. It's harder for the chronically sick, who after time, become adjusted to their limitations. With God all things are possible, however.*

*When a person has a long-term illness or condition, is it easy to keep on hoping and believing for a healing? No, it's not easy, but it can be done with the help of the Lord and the promises that are in His Word. It all depends on what we focus on. What Scriptures are we meditating on? 2 Corinthians 5:7 says, "For we walk by faith, not by sight." Focus on verses about the One who took stripes for everyone, so that all could be made whole.*

\* \* \* \* \* \* \*

Jesus ignored the man's excuse. He must have surprised the lame man when He boldly said, "Rise, take up your bed and walk!" Think about the enabling power behind those words! It wasn't three days later or even three hours later that the man could finally muster enough strength to stand up. His miracle was immediate! He was no longer a cripple! His legs were made strong and well at the commanding words of Jesus! He immediately took up his bed and walked! An Amazing Miracle!

## Selah . . . Pause and Reflect

*In John 6:63, Jesus says that His words are Spirit and Life. The words of Jesus are powerful! We can speak out the promises in the Bible, believing they are true for us today. We can put our name in Bible promises; owning them for ourselves. Jesus showed the lame man His goodness.*

*Heart check: Jesus wants to demonstrate His goodness to us as well! He is no respecter of persons. He loves all of us the same. He is looking to give His life-giving power to the ones who will believe His Word. This miracle lets us know that healing a chronic infirmity is not a problem for Jesus! Up until Jesus came, the man pictured himself as "the lame man." Jesus gave him a new picture of who he was when He said, "Rise and*

*Walk!" Then he became that new picture! How do we picture ourselves? Healed and Whole!*

\* \* \* \* \* \*

The day this man's healing took place was the Sabbath, a day of rest. Jesus came to demonstrate that helping people on that day was much more important than obeying the petty, man-made guidelines that were so important to the Pharisees, but had no connection to the original intent of God's Sabbath Law.

These leaders saw the man walking along carrying his sleeping mat. They could have said, "Hey man, you're walking! That's wonderful!" But instead, they told him that it was a Sabbath day and he had no business to carry his bed! Most likely with stern faces, they reminded him that he was breaking the Law!

The healed man spoke up and said, "It's not my fault, I was told to take up my mat and walk." Of course, the religious Jews would not let it go; they wanted to know who told him to do that. However, Jesus had slipped away before revealing who He was to the man.

## Selah . . . Pause and Reflect

*Jesus was always motivated by love. We can be too, looking for ways to bless and encourage someone. (Romans 5:5).*

*Heart check: What are the priorities of Jesus? When we read through the gospels, we see that Jesus always wanted to help people. John 3:16 tells us that "God so loved the world that He gave..." First He give TO us, then He gives THROUGH us.*

\* \* \* \* \* \* \*

Later, Jesus found the man in the temple, and He said to him, "Look at you now! You're healed! Make sure that you walk away from any sin. You don't want something worse to come upon you."

John 3:17 says, "For God did not send His Son into the world to condemn the world, but that the world through Him might be saved." Jesus did not make a habit of saying something about a person's sins. Why did He point this out? Could it mean that Jesus wants us to experience His abundant life, not only in our healed body, but also in our cleansed soul?

## Selah . . . Pause and Reflect

*To have a victorious life, it's important to keep our heart clean. The still small voice of the Spirit will give us a warning - watch your attitude!*

*Do you think that things like resentment, bitterness, taking offense, self-pity, unforgiveness and hatred in our soul can make a difference and affect our physical body? When we continually carry some of those things, it surely does affect our joy and peace level! Perhaps this man at the pool had to lay down some bitterness, self-pity and the rest. Then his heart would be clean and healed, the same as his body. Joy and hatred can't stay together in our heart. They don't mix. The hatred has to go for us to have joy.*

*Heart check: Jesus is the Best! He points out the things we tolerate in our soul that are actually harmful for us. He takes us by the hand and lets us know He is right with us to help us overcome any of these negative things. We have Him living inside, always loving us, always wanting the best for us, always giving us inner strength and support.*

\* \* \* \* \* \*

After his encounter with Jesus at the temple, the man found the Jewish leaders and told them Who it was that healed him on the Sabbath. From then on, the Jews began to carefully watch Jesus regarding what He did on the Sabbath.

## Selah . . . Pause and Reflect

*It is interesting that Jesus was loving people and helping them. The religious Jews were hateful and wanted to kill a person - Jesus! What a contrast of hearts and motives! What a difference in their thinking! Life and death, love and hate.*

*These men must have thought that God would be pleased if they got rid of this evil Person who did not abide by the Sabbath rules. They didn't realize what the Father was really like. They could have just looked at Jesus to see the heart of the Heavenly Father. They missed it, didn't they?!*

*Heart check: When we pursue love, make love our aim, (1 Corinthians 14:1), we end up partnering with God to do His works.*

\* \* \* \* \* \*

*WHO IS JESUS FOR US TODAY?*

*Jesus freely gives us ABUNDANT LIFE!*

*He puts His Love in our hearts.*

\* \* \* \* \* \* \*

*WHAT DID WE LEARN FROM THIS STORY?*

*Focus on Jesus to heal you. He is the Savior who brings healing and health to the whole human race.*

*Don't make excuses! Do something about your situation! To see miracles, it helps to have desire.*

*Desire comes from being in the Word, meditating on the promises of God and counting on them for ourselves.*

*Jesus only did what He saw His Father doing. This is a good example for us. Listen for His still small voice.*

*This story can encourage a friend who has suffered a long time with an infirmity. With Jesus, there is hope. All things are possible with Him!*

# WITHERED HAND HEALED

Matthew 12:9-14          Mark 3:1-6          Luke 6:6-11

*Luke 6:6 Now it happened on another Sabbath, that He entered the synagogue and taught. And a man was there whose right hand was withered.*

The Bible records several times that Jesus performed a cure on the Sabbath. Most of the locations were at a synagogue, which is the center of community life for God's people. The Sabbath was to remember and commemorate the completion of Creation. God finished His perfect work in six days and then He rested. God gave the Sabbath to be a day of blessing and rest for man. (Genesis 2:2-3).

Sickness was not God's design in creation. Adam and Eve knew nothing of sickness. It was only after their disobedience and sin did sickness come into the world. They gave their authority to rule the earth over to the devil.

Jesus came to undo the works of the devil, (1 John 3:8), which included sickness. To bring healing to a hurting person on the Sabbath seemed so right and good, a restoration to the original creation. The scribes and Pharisees didn't see it that way. They had made strict laws about "work."

## Selah . . . Pause and Reflect

*What if the man with the withered hand was a brick layer by trade? He could not do his job if his hand was crippled.*

*In those days there were no agencies like we have now, that would help disabled people financially. This man's life must have been difficult, especially if he had a family to provide for. We are told that it is his right hand that was not useable. Most people use their right hand for many things, including eating and writing.*

*Heart Check: The heart of Jesus was to bring healing and restoration to anyone who needed it. He was concerned about doing good and blessing someone. We can do the same! Be Jesus, especially to hurting people. We need each other. Little encouragements count big!*

\* \* \* \* \* \* \*

The scribes and Pharisees were there, watching closely to see if Jesus would heal on a Sabbath day. They were eager to find a reason to accuse Him for breaking Jewish laws. They believed that doing something to cause a healing was to "work."

They asked Jesus, "is it lawful to work on the Sabbath?" Jesus answered them with a question. "What man is there among you who has one sheep, and if it falls into a pit on the Sabbath, will not lay hold of it and lift it out? Of how much more value then is a man than a sheep? Therefore, it is lawful to do good on the Sabbath."

## Selah . . . Pause and Reflect

*Jesus knew the Law better than they did! He said, "The Sabbath was made for man, and not man for the Sabbath." (Mark 2:27).*

*God's Law was never intended to be interpreted the way the Pharisees did. They believed that healing was not allowed on the Sabbath, except when there was danger to life. Even then, measures could be taken only to prevent the condition from getting worse, nothing could be done to improve the condition.*

*<u>Heart Check:</u> The religious leaders and scholars were trained in the Law and had accepted it as being truth. They not only held to the Law that Moses wrote, but also to the 613 additional "rules" that the religious leadership added over the years. Those laws became such a part of their belief system they felt they must enforce each one of them, even to the point of taking the life of anyone who disagreed with them. The teachings of the Bible are always the final authority for our beliefs.*

\* \* \* \* \* \*

Jesus knew the thoughts of the scribes and Pharisees, that they were looking for an occasion to catch Him in the act of healing on the Sabbath so they could accuse Him and have the proof!

They thought Jesus would lay His hands on someone. That would have been interpreted as work. This time He simply had the man do all the work! Jesus didn't even walk towards the man, He told him to come and stand by Him. Then He told the man to stretch forth his hand and the healing took place without Jesus doing any work! The man's hand was restored as whole as the other when he stretched it out!

## Selah . . . Pause and Reflect

*Jesus came to bring light and truth to all of us, including to those who made outlandish rules for God's people. He came to set the Pharisees free from petty rules! He sets us free as well! He demonstrated that the Father's heart was to do good and to help people, no matter what day of the week it was.*

*Jesus made it easy for a person to use their own faith to cooperate with their miracle. In this case, the man had to stretch out his withered hand. He had to do something that was impossible. As he went ahead and obeyed what Jesus said to do, the miracle happened. Faith, in this case, was not waiting for something to happen; it was doing something, believing it would happen.*

*Jesus did not have one technique or form for us to follow when He prayed for the sick. He was led by the Father as far as the "how." Each time we read healings in the Bible, we see they are a bit different from each other.*

*Heart Check: The man listened to what Jesus said to do. I can imagine the man's gaze was kept on the face of Jesus. He must have seen tremendous compassion and warmth. There is something so compelling and powerful about love. We trust people we know for sure that love us.*

*The man not only listened, but he was obedient. He walked to where Jesus was. He stretched out his hand. He saw his hand restored! How wonderful for him that Jesus gave him*

*the use of this important part of his body! What a gift! Jesus*
*gave him back his life! Can you imagine how grateful he was?!*

\* \* \* \* \* \* \*

The religious bunch were filled with rage! They didn't like being outsmarted by Jesus! They were so sure they could bring charges against Him this time. Nope. Not happening. It wasn't His time. The man did all the "work."

They missed seeing Who it was that was in their midst. They had no idea that Jesus, the Son of Man, was the Lord of the Sabbath. (Mark 2:28). The Sabbath is the Lord's Day, which meant Jesus was equal with God.

The Pharisees went out and plotted against Him, how they might destroy Him.

## Selah . . . Pause and Reflect

*Earlier, Jesus asked the scribes and Pharisees, "Is it lawful on the Sabbath to do good or to do evil, to save life or to kill?" They kept silent. Wow. When Jesus looked around at them, He was grieved by the hardness of their hearts. It was a simple question with a simple correct answer!*

*It's hard to imagine how anyone can get to the point where they prefer that someone doing good should die, simply because the good they are doing is done on the wrong day! This story tells about a man whose life and livelihood were restored to him and there was no rejoicing over that by the religious crowd. Only a fresh resolve to find out how to take the life of Jesus.*

*Heart Check:* *We must beware of some serious stumbling blocks in our faith walk. For example, pride. "It's my way or the highway!" Jealousy and envy will take us down for sure. Even our words can bring life or death. (Proverbs 18:21). The Pharisees thought they were defending God's ways, when they were actually at odds with His ways. God is always about goodness and love.*

\* \* \* \* \* \*

## WHO IS JESUS FOR US TODAY?

*Jesus is our RESTORER! Jesus gave the man his life back!*

*He makes all things new and beautiful.*

\* \* \* \* \* \*

## WHAT DID WE LEARN FROM THIS STORY?

*Jesus knew He would have opposition in the synagogue, but He went anyway because He cared for the people.*

*Sometimes Faith and Activity go together!
Stretch forth your hand!*

*The doctrine we hold dear must have the same spirit of love and grace that Jesus had.
Listen to God! Do what He says! Sometimes faith is not waiting for something to happen; it is obeying God, believing it will happen.*

*Jesus' healing ministry happened many times where God's people enjoyed being part of a community in a synagogue on the Sabbath.*

# CENTURION'S
# SERVANT HEALED

## Matthew 8:5-13    Luke 7:1-10

*Matthew 8:5-6 Now when Jesus had entered Capernaum, a centurion came to Him, pleading with Him, saying, "Lord, my servant is lying at home paralyzed, dreadfully tormented."*

A centurion was a Roman officer who had authority over 100 soldiers. He was stationed in Israel to subject the Jews to the Emperor's rule. Rome was the ruling power in Israel during the time of Jesus. A centurion would have had a pagan upbringing. Most Romans looked down on the Jews and took pleasure in running their lives.

This centurion was unique because he genuinely cared about his servant. This kind of compassion was not the norm among centurions. Servants could be viewed simply as slaves with no regard for them as valuable persons. The centurion begged Jesus to heal his servant, an indication of his empathy for and his devotion to the servant. It also showed his trust in Jesus to heal.

## Selah . . . Pause and Reflect

*It would be normal in that society to look at any servant as simply being the property of the master, nothing more. The centurion obviously had a genuine love for and friendship with the sick man.*

*When Jesus was rejected by the people of his home town Nazareth, He spent a lot of time in Capernaum. This city became His base and He performed miracles there. The centurion could have even witnessed some of those miracles or talked to ones who were healed. He was confident that Jesus was able to heal his servant.*

*Heart Check: How do we see people? Are there people we regard more important because of what they do or what they have? Jesus doesn't do that, He loves us all the same. It is amazing this centurion, who had power and authority, also had such a loving, Christ-like attitude toward his servant.*

\* \* \* \* \* \* \*

Jesus told the centurion that He would come and heal his servant. The response He got surprised Him! The centurion answered and said, "Lord, I am not worthy that You should come under my roof. But only speak a word, and my servant will be healed. I am a man under authority, having soldiers under me. I say to this one, go, and he goes; and to another, come, and he comes; and to my servant, do this, and he does it."

## Selah . . . Pause and Reflect

*This centurion was a humble man. That in itself is unusual. It's easy for most people to be proud when they rise to leadership in their profession. He said he was not worthy of a visit from this Man of God.*

*The centurion expressed his faith in Jesus by telling Him to simply speak a word, and his servant would be healed! He was convinced that Jesus had supernatural healing power resident in Him and that He was able to use that power to heal people, even at a distance.*

*Being a centurion, he would daily give orders to soldiers who were under his command; telling one to go and another to come. They responded in obedience. He also told his servants to do something and they would do it. He understood authority and how to use it.*

*Heart Check: This man believed that Jesus had all authority over any kind of sickness. We can adopt the same mindset. When we speak a verse in the Bible in the name of Jesus, that Word carries an authority with it. He sent His Word and it healed them. (Psalm 107:20).*

\* \* \* \* \* \* \*

Jesus came to preach primarily to the Jews. Jesus listened to this humble, faith-filled man speak and He marveled! He said, "I have not found such great faith, not even in Israel!" Obviously, the centurion man was not Jewish, He was a Gentile.

## *Selah . . . Pause and Reflect*

*The early church held to the concept of the Jewish people being the only ones who would have eternal life. It wasn't until Peter had a vision about clean and unclean that the elders knew Jesus came for the whole world. Jesus died on the cross for the salvation of all mankind. Think of how many non-Jews you know that are part of the family of God!*

*This centurion will go down in history as being one of only two people mentioned in the Bible that Jesus commended for their faith. (The other was the Canaanite woman whose daughter was healed of a demon.) Do you think this man must have treasured in his heart these encouraging words from Jesus? Sure.*

*Heart Check: The kingdom of God is not advanced when we criticize each other or think we are better than others. The kingdom is advanced when we believe God's Word is true and we love all people.*

\* \* \* \* \* \* \*

Then Jesus said to the centurion, "Go your way; and as you have believed, so let it be done for you." (Matthew 8:13). And his servant was healed that same hour.

## Selah . . . Pause and Reflect

*This story is about a man who was a Roman officer. He was probably the most unlikely kind of person to have qualities such as: Love, Humility, Faith and Authority. This story reveals the heart of this man and all of these qualities are evident. Pretty amazing!*

*Heart Check: It is through our trials that we get a chance to develop faith. This man gets an A+ for learning how to believe God for a miracle! Do you think that he asked Jesus to be his Savior? How could he not do, after having such a powerful encounter with Jesus?!*

*Did he organize a Home Group, maybe made up of fellow Roman believers? Together that group saw many people healed and set free! Fun to use our imagination! I'm sure this centurion had a wonderful life after his time spent with*

*Jesus! What do you think? When we meet him in heaven, let's ask him to share with us...the rest of the story!*

\* \* \* \* \* \* \*

## WHO IS JESUS FOR US TODAY?

*Jesus honors FAITH from whoever has it.*

*He grants healing to those who dare to believe Him for it.*

\* \* \* \* \* \* \*

## WHAT DID WE LEARN FROM THIS STORY?

*Love and help those who can't pay us back.*

*Refuse to be proud. The Lord exalts the humble.*

*The Word of God has both power and authority.*

*The centurion humbled himself before Jesus. Twice he referred to Jesus as "Lord." (Matthew 8:6,8).*

*Use our trial to build our faith! Saturate ourselves with the promises of God.*

*"Go your way; and as you have believed, so let it be done for you." (Jesus)*

*Love - Humility - Faith - Authority*

# WIDOW OF NAIN'S SON

## Luke 7:11-17

*Luke 7:11-12 Now it happened that He went into a village called Nain; and many of His disciples went with Him, and a large crowd. And when He came near the gate of the village, behold, a dead man was being carried out, the only son of his mother; and she was a widow. And a large crowd from the village was with her.*

Nain was a small village south of Capernaum. As Jesus approached the village, He met a funeral procession on their way to the cemetery.

## Selah . . . Pause and Reflect

*It was no accident that Jesus arrived at Nain right when this funeral procession was going out of the village to bury this young man's body. Jesus did not arrive an hour too early or an hour too late! This was a divine appointment for Jesus.*

*Heart Check: Do we notice divine appointments in our busy lives? Do we believe that God can use us to be an encouragement to someone? Or, maybe He wants us to connect with someone who will encourage us. We all have had those divine appointments happen, haven't we?*

\* \* \* \* \* \*

This grieving mother had just lost her only son. Her husband was also dead, so she was now left to fend for herself. In those days, life would not be easy for a woman on her own. She would lack the protection and provision that a man could provide for her. Besides losing the son she loved so much, she faced an uncertain future. What would become of her? Even now, fear began creeping into her thoughts. Soon she would be dealing with loneliness and hopelessness. How could she cope?

## Selah . . . Pause and Reflect

*Put yourself in her place. Women in those days were not trained for employment, like women of today are. Israel did not have Social Security or an official government program to financially help the underprivileged. Hopefully, she may have had a sibling or kind neighbor who would look out for her and make sure she had food.*

*Heart Check: Do you know anyone in her situation? Perhaps an elderly neighbor lady who would love a sample of your famous chicken soup!*

\* \* \* \* \* \* \*

When Jesus saw the mother weeping, He felt deep compassion for her. He told her to stop crying. Then He went to the open coffin and the pallbearers stopped. Jesus spoke to the body, "Young man, I say to you, arise and live!"

Immediately, the young man sat up and began speaking! Jesus then presented him to his mother. Wow! Amazing!

## Selah . . . Pause and Reflect

*Picture this whole scene in your mind as if you were there. What a black and white difference in everyone's emotions, especially for the Mom! She went from sobbing with grief to wiping happy tears off her cheeks! She has her arm around her son and she could feel his strong arm around her shoulder.*

*<u>Heart Check:</u> The story tells us that there was a multitude of people who followed along in this funeral procession. This woman and her son were obviously loved by a whole lot of towns-people. What if someone shouted - Let's celebrate! We'll sing praises to God and have a feast to welcome this young man back to life! Israeli men like to dance joyfully in a circle. Women in a circle too! Party Time! Let's celebrate what God did through His prophet! The report about how Jesus raised this young man back to life went throughout Judea and all the surrounding region.*

\* \* \* \* \* \* \*

Many people witnessed this young man be raised from the dead. The people from the town and also the crowd that followed Jesus were all struck with a holy sense of awe. They shouted praises to God, saying, "A great prophet has risen among us."

## Selah . . . Pause and Reflect

*They immediately gave God praise for this miracle. They believed that Jesus was a "prophet" sent by God. Perhaps they recalled how two Old Testament prophets restored dead sons to their mothers. (Elijah - 1 Kings 17:17-24 and Elisha - 2 Kings 4:32-37).*

*<u>Heart Check:</u> Jesus and the mother are the focus of this story. The only thing we are told about the son is that he sat up and began speaking. We are not even told what he said!*

*The thing to notice is how Jesus felt when he saw the mother weeping. His heart was stirred with compassion. He feels that same compassion toward us when we are grieving in some way. He is not aloof and uncaring. We can tell Him just how we feel. He will give comfort and breathe life into our situation.*

\* \* \* \* \* \* \*

## *WHO IS JESUS FOR US TODAY?*

*Jesus has COMPASSION for anyone who is grieving.*

*He cares deeply for anyone who is hurting.*

\* \* \* \* \* \* \*

## *WHAT DID WE LEARN FROM THIS STORY?*

*Jesus carried the Father's authority to cause even "life" to come upon a dead body. The Prince of Life met Death at the city gate and Life won!*

*When Jesus saw the grieving mother, His heart broke for her. He tenderly said to her, Please don't cry.*

*The people reacted with a holy awe and worship, saying that God had visited His people.*

*The news of this miracle traveled fast throughout Judea and the surrounding region! No need for cell phones back then!*

# GADARENE DEMONIAC

## Matthew 8:28-34    Mark 5:1-20    Luke 8:26-39

*Luke 8:26-27 Then they sailed to the country of the Gadarenes, which is opposite Galilee. And when He stepped out on the land, there met Him a certain man from the city who had demons for a long time. And he wore no clothes, nor did he live in a house but in the tombs.*

## Selah . . . Pause and Reflect

*The tombs this man lived in were caves used to bury the dead. Night and day he was in the mountains and caves crying out and cutting himself with stones. The people in the surrounding cities had put chains and shackles on him to try to tame him. He simply pulled the chains apart and broke the shackles! Everyone knew who this man was.*

*Heart Check: It was evening when Jesus and the disciples got into the boat to sail across the Sea of Galilee to the country of the Gadarenes. They encountered a violent storm with high winds. While Jesus was sleeping, the disciples bailed water and feared for their lives. When they woke Jesus up, He calmed the storm and they were safe. When they landed on the far shore in the dead of night, I can imagine the twelve were still trying to recover from that near death experience! Then, to have a naked, demonized man running toward them, yelling as he came, must have been rather unnerving for the disciples! Can you picture yourself being there?*

\* \* \* \* \* \*

Matthew's account tells us there were two demon-possessed men coming out of the tombs. They were exceedingly fierce, so that no one could pass that way. Mark and Luke write about one man. Perhaps they chose to emphasize the one who was more prominent.

When the man saw Jesus, he fell at His feet, and with a loud voice he cried out, begging to not be tormented before the time.

## Selah . . . Pause and Reflect

*It is interesting to note that demons knew who Jesus was without any introduction! (Unlike spiritually blind religious rulers in Israel!) The demons cried out - "What have we to do with You, Jesus, Son of The Most High God? Have You come here to torment us before the time?" The demons feared being thrown into the abyss before the Day of Judgment.*

*Heart Check: Satan's crowd knows full well that a day is coming when Satan and all of his demons will be judged by the Lord Who has All Power. How many people do you know that are not aware of a coming Day of Judgment for all mankind as well as for the demon hordes? Or, perhaps friends and family know there is a time when God will give rewards and judgments, but that truth has been overshadowed by the cares of life and forgotten.*

\* \* \* \* \* \*

Jesus told the unclean spirits to come out of the man. They were stubborn and did not want to leave! Jesus asked the man what his name was. He answered saying, "My name is Legion; for we are many." Then the demons began begging Jesus to send them into the pigs that were feeding there near the mountains.

## Selah . . . Pause and Reflect

*A Roman Legion at full strength consisted of 6,000 troops. You can decide if the man had that many demons! He must have had at least 2,000 demons to be able to enter into that many pigs that were nearby. It's mind boggling to picture a human being in that desperate state. How did he get that way?*

*Pigs were unclean to Jews, but they were revered in pagan rites. The whole Gentile region of the Gadarenes had shrines to Baal and other pagan gods.*

*Heart Check: This man was in a helpless, hopeless state with a miserable life! Those demons took over his mind, his actions and his voice. Basically, he did not have a life. The demons controlled him.*

*Jesus didn't see him as a complete wreck of a person who should be avoided at all costs. Jesus saw a man suffering greatly who wanted to be free and normal.*

\* \* \* \* \* \* \*

Jesus gave the demons permission to enter into the swine. When they did, the entire herd ran down the hill into the Sea of Galilee and drowned! When those who fed the pigs saw what happened, they ran and told the owners of the pigs that a "whole lot of money just drowned in the sea!" People from the area came to see for themselves what had happened. When they saw the demonized man was dressed and calmly sitting at the feet of Jesus, they could hardly believe their eyes! They didn't expect anything like that to happen and it was totally overwhelming. They really did not like the part about such a big financial loss. That was extremely disturbing! They told Jesus He was responsible for their losses and He was not welcome there! He had better leave, like now!

## Selah . . . Pause and Reflect

*The pig owners were very concerned about assets and profit. (Just think of what it would be like for us if all the banks closed suddenly and without warning!) The people from the surrounding area didn't seem to care much about the amazing change in the demonic man. The Bible says that when they saw him clothed and in his right mind, they were afraid. (Mark 5:15).*

*Heart Check: People living in the country of the Gadarenes did not know the one true God. We are different because we know we have a God who loves us and is well able to take good care of us! God's Word helps us learn how we are to react if we ever do go through difficult times. "Seek first the kingdom of God and His righteousness, and all these things (food and apparel) shall be added to you." (Matthew 6:33).*

\* \* \* \* \* \* \*

The man, from whom the demons had departed, begged Jesus that he might be with Him. Jesus told him to go to his own house and talk about how God has changed him. The man went his way and proclaimed throughout the whole city what great things God has done for him! Two contrasts are given in this story: a picture of the man before and after, and also a picture of him begging to stay with Jesus and the people begging Jesus to go!

## Selah . . . Pause and Reflect

*This man experienced such genuine love coming from Jesus that it changed his life! Perhaps he had never experienced real love. Love is powerful and it must have brought a tremendous amount of healing to his soul. No wonder he would want to bask in that kind of love daily by being in the presence of Jesus. Can you blame him for wanting to be the thirteenth disciple of Jesus?*

*<u>Heart Check:</u> Jesus came to this area only once, never to return. The Father directed His Son to cross the lake that night (knowing there would be a storm), to bring healing and wholeness to one man. The Father not only loved and cared for that man who was in such a desperate situation, He loved the multitude of Gentile people in that pagan region who would hear the message of God's love and healing power! Jesus not only set this man free from demons, but sent him out as a missionary to tell his testimony to his countrymen. He was the first "sent one" to evangelize a region! Later Jesus sent the disciples out two-by-two. (Matthew 10:5).*

\* \* \* \* \* \*

## WHO IS JESUS FOR US TODAY?

*Jesus CARES DEEPLY for society's throw-away people.*

*His power to restore and heal is unlimited!*

\* \* \* \* \* \* \*

## *WHAT DID WE LEARN FROM THIS STORY?*

*Society was powerless to help this man or tame
him with chains, so they rejected him.*

*This story is about the compassion of Christ and His obedience
to the divine guidance of His Father. He crossed the lake at the
risk of their lives to rescue one man.*

*Every person created in the image of God has worth,
no matter how depraved they may be.*

*Do we need to guard against having wrong priorities? Do
we cherish our bank account more than helping people?*

*Can we see people like Jesus does? We don't see a wreck of a
person, but someone who can be transformed by Jesus.*

*Jesus saw him as a man set free! His testimony would bring many
to a knowledge of God. They all knew him "before
Jesus" and now could see him "after Jesus!"*

# WOMAN WITH ISSUE
# OF BLOOD

Matthew 9:20-22      Mark 5:25-34      Luke 8:43-48

*Mark 5:25-26 Now a certain woman had a flow of blood for twelve years, and had suffered many things from many physicians. She had spent all that she had and was no better, but rather grew worse.*

For twelve years this woman was shunned by society because of her uncleanness. According to Laws given by Moses, this woman was not supposed to be in public places. She was an outcast, possibly living alone and having to fend for herself. This was an especially vulnerable position for a woman on her own. She had no father or husband to speak up for her and protect her.

## Selah . . . Pause and Reflect

*Think about what a difficult life this woman lived, and for so long. Every bed or chair she used would have been made unclean. Anyone touching that bed or chair was required to wash their clothes and bathe themselves. They would be unclean until evening. (Leviticus 15:25-30). Anyone accidentally touching her or her clothes would be unclean. Because of this, even her family may have rejected her! What an emotional blow that would have been.*

*She was not allowed to attend synagogue or any public gathering. This would have made her unable to receive the teachings of the Rabbis or to have fellowship with anyone who could encourage her. She suffered scorn and loneliness. She must have felt desperation and discouragement. It was a common belief in those days that people having serious physical issues, like a constant flow of blood, were being punished by God. That surely didn't help her feel good about herself! Constant disdain and rejection would make anyone feel worthless.*

*Heart Check: Anyone who has suffered from a long-term disease or difficult situation can easily identify with this woman. Hopelessness can creep in and also discouragement. Jesus and His Word give hope, healing and encouragement! During those dark days, look to Him and the promises of His Word. Jesus wants us to learn to trust Him. He knows our situation and He wants to help us. Nothing is impossible for Him!*

\* \* \* \* \* \* \*

Did God make sure this woman crossed paths with someone who had experienced a life-changing miracle by the hands of Jesus? Maybe someone like the crippled man who sat for 38 years at the Pool of Bethesda. Let's imagine that man told her it wasn't the pool that cured him, it was Jesus! She heard that Jesus was willing to heal anyone and that He had compassion on the sick. She was greatly encouraged! Hope rose up in her and she decided to risk being in public.

She pictured herself getting healed by Jesus. She began to say to herself over and over, "If only I could touch the hem of His clothes, I will be healed." That was her point of contact to receive a miracle. That declaration became more firm and urgent inside of her each day.

When she learned that Jesus had come to her area, she made plans to get to Him at any cost. She must have taken a deep breath when she saw how large the crowd was and how many people were pressing close to Jesus.

## Selah . . . Pause and Reflect

*Because of the healing testimony she heard, she gained confidence that healing could be hers as well! She refused to think that Jesus would deny her the miracle she sought from Him. (That's faith!) She must have come to understand that Jesus came from God. It was the unlimited power of God that worked through Him to accomplish these amazing works.*

*<u>Heart Check:</u> It is very beneficial when we share a testimony of something God did for us. It strengthens our own faith for the next miracle. It also encourages others to believe for their miracle. "If God did it for you, He will do it for me. He's no respecter of persons." (Acts 10:34). It also is beneficial to picture ourselves healed, like she did. Speak out Scriptures that tell us God's will concerning healing. We can picture Him being faithful to heal us!*

\* \* \* \* \* \* \*

Doctors had failed her. She was convinced that Jesus was now the only source of the healing she longed for. She was determined to press through the crowd! It wasn't easy because there were some that seemed irritated as she went ahead of them. She didn't care. She knew she was taking a risk. No matter, it would be worth it all when she was healed! She kept her focus on the back of Jesus' head and made her way towards Him.

She hoped no one would notice, especially Jesus, and she could quickly slip away after she was made whole. If people in the crowd knew about her flow of blood, she would be shamed and rejected for being unclean. Most likely, she would also be in trouble with the Jewish religious authorities for being in a public place.

## Selah . . . Pause and Reflect

*This woman was desperate! She was willing to take a big risk. Her life had been going downhill for twelve years and she saw no relief in sight. That is, until she heard about Jesus. She learned how He healed everyone who came to Him. When she found out about this miracle-working Man of God, it changed everything for her! Hope sprung up in her heart.*

*Heart Check: The facts of her situation, the abnormal flow of blood, did not consume her thinking anymore. She now took hold of truths that were higher than facts: Jesus is her Healer! She was not denying that she had the flow of blood. She chose to believe that the power residing in Jesus would cure the problem. She was also convinced that He was more than willing to share that power with her!*

\* \* \* \* \* \* \*

The multitude walking with Jesus were simply onlookers. In contrast, this woman came for one reason, to touch Him and to receive her healing. She knew she was breaking a Jewish Law and wanted simply to get her healing and leave before she bothered Jesus or had to explain anything. When she touched the hem of His robe, she felt in her body that her condition was healed!

Jesus knew immediately that power had gone out of Him. He turned around in the crowd and said, "Who touched My clothes?"

The disciples reminded Him that so many were pressing against Him. Why would He even ask such a question?!

## Selah . . . Pause and Reflect

*Jesus said, "Somebody touched Me, for I perceived power going out from Me." The disciples perceived in the natural realm the jostling of the crowd touching Him. The sense of healing power he felt leaving His body was in the supernatural realm.*

\* \* \* \* \* \*

<u>Heart Check:</u> *This miracle taught the disciples and the onlookers that the power to heal was resident in Jesus. A healing miracle could be manifested for anyone who believed Jesus was merciful and kind, full of healing power and willing to help in time of need. In this incident, Jesus did not even know who put a demand on that healing anointing.*

\* \* \* \* \* \*

Jesus looked around and saw the woman who had just been healed. When the woman knew that she was not hidden, she came trembling and fell down in front of Jesus. She then told him the reason she came and that she felt in her body that she was now healed.

Jesus said to her, "Daughter, be of good cheer, your faith has made you well. Go in peace." He wanted her to realize that it wasn't because she touched the hem of His garment that He would heal her. It was because she was convinced in her mind and heart that He simply had the ability and the willingness to heal. Her faith released His power!

## Selah . . . Pause and Reflect

*She realized she could not stay anonymous, so she came trembling to Jesus. That tells us that she was willing to push through her fears and be vulnerable and honest in front of Jesus. She was so grateful to be "clean" now! Falling before Him would indicate her worship and thanksgiving.*

*Confession was humbling, but necessary for her. Coming forward and confessing out loud in public was very scary for her, but she did it anyway. She was rewarded with the comforting words of Jesus, "Daughter of Mine, your faith has made you well." Do you think those words were quickly forgotten? NO! Those healing, life-giving words would echo in her thoughts throughout her entire life. She could feel God's love in every words spoken by Jesus. The scary experience of revealing herself in front of the crowd turned out to be a tremendous blessing, giving her confidence for her future and the assurance of the love and approval of the the only One Who really mattered!*

*Jesus said, "Go in peace." The message those words gave was that she would never have to deal with this horrible condition ever again!*

*Heart Check: Jesus called her "daughter." That must have healed a huge wound in her soul, having been probably shunned by her family because of her unclean state. Jesus was saying that she was now HIS daughter and He was happy about that! She also knew that her own father would not reject her anymore, now that she was cured and "clean." Her life was forever changed! Now she had a life!*

*Many years before the time Jesus began His ministry, the religious community used various Laws to isolate "unclean" people. These people must have felt estranged from God Himself. Jesus demonstrated God's desire to draw near to the unclean and make them whole. This woman and the lepers mentioned in the Bible were all considered "unclean." Jesus loved on all of them with Father's Love. The ones that people rejected, Jesus embraced and loved.*

\* \* \* \* \* \*

## *WHO IS JESUS FOR US TODAY?*

*Jesus makes us CLEAN AND WHOLE.*

*He meets emotional needs; He calls us His Son/Daughter.*

\* \* \* \* \* \*

## *WHAT DID WE LEARN FROM THIS STORY?*

*Be courageous in what you believe! Don't be swayed by circumstances or discouraged by others.*

*Let's not be like the crowd that simply followed Jesus, expecting nothing from Him, getting nothing!*

*Don't wait for Jesus to find us! The Bible says there is healing power in Jesus and the Word. We will have it!*

*Jesus gives His complete attention to anyone who believes He can and will meet their need.*

*Healing affects every area of our life!*

# DAUGHTER OF JAIRUS RESTORED

Matthew 9:18-26        Mark 5:22-43        Luke 8:41-56

*Luke 8:41-42 And behold, there came a man named Jairus, and he was a ruler of the synagogue. And he fell down at Jesus' feet and begged Him to come to his house, for he had an only daughter about twelve years of age, and she was dying.*

The night before this story begins, a demonized man was set free by Jesus on the east side of Sea the of Galilee. In the morning, Jesus and His disciples went to the west side of the lake, being greeted by a large crowd. Jesus was well-known in that area of The Galilee, having done many miracles there.

Think about the timing of these events. Do you think Jesus and the disciples got much sleep that previous night? Did they bring along food with them? Maybe. On arrival in the morning, they were immediately put into a position of meeting people's needs. Jesus always put the needs of people above His own. How often did such a situation happen? Perhaps many times.

Jairus was the leader of the local Jewish congregation. He was an important man in that community, most likely known and respected by everyone. He forgot about his status and influence as he humbled himself, kneeling before Jesus in respect. At the moment, the only thing on his mind was his darling daughter who was critically ill.

## Selah . . . Pause and Reflect

*Jairus was a godly family man. He obviously had a deep love for his wife and only daughter, who was twelve. The idea of his daughter possibly dying was unthinkable to him! When He heard Jesus was in the area, he searched until he found Him. He was a desperate father, trusting the One known to be a Healer would come to his house and perform a miracle. It's probable that Jairus had heard of the healings done by Jesus and perhaps he witnessed one or more. He already had confidence that Jesus could and would make his daughter well again.*

*<u>Heart Check:</u> Do we have that same confidence in Jesus that Jairus had? We can meditate on healing Scriptures, putting our name in each one. (Psalm 107:20). We can also look at what the Word says about the faithfulness of God to perform His Word. (Hebrews 10:23). We can ponder the Love that Jesus had for us when He took those brutal stripes so we can be healed. (1 Peter 2:24).*

\* \* \* \* \* \*

By the time Jairus found Jesus, there was a big crowd, all wanting to be near Him. Jairus was determined! Even it if took effort, with a little pushing and shoving, he was going to get to Jesus! He would ask, even beg, Jesus to come to his house.

## Selah . . . Pause and Reflect

*The determination of Jairus had a lot to do with how much he loved his daughter. Because of that love and fatherly devotion to care for her, He would stop at nothing to see her well again! Jesus walked in the power of God and He would lay hands on her and bring a healing. Jairus knew it!*

*Heart Check: Do we get weary in our prayer time, quitting before we see the answer? Let's be like Jairus, who did not give up! Does love motivate us?*

\* \* \* \* \* \* \*

Jesus agreed to go to the home of Jairus. As they walked along, Jairus was encouraged because things were looking up! But wait! What is happening?!

A woman came behind Jesus and touched the hem of His garment. Jesus turned around and looked for who it was. He said that virtue had gone out of Him! Then He and the woman had a conversation.

Jairus thought, "This is not happening! We cannot delay, time is of the utmost importance right now!" Then men came and said that the girl had died. Those who brought the news were convinced that death was final, nothing more could be done for her. A miracle was outside the realm of possibilities at this point. "There's no need to trouble the Master any longer, your daughter has died. We're sorry for your loss, Jairus, let's go now."

## *Selah . . . Pause and Reflect*

*It was assumed that once a person stopped breathing for a length of time; that person was dead and could not be resuscitated. A man did come back to life when his body touched the bones of Elisha! (2 Kings 13:20-21). But, that was in a different category than what normal people could*

74

*do! That had everything to do with who Elisha was, a man of God, a prophet who was known for seeing miracles done by God through his life and ministry.*

*<u>Heart Check:</u> The men coming with the news of the girl's death did not discern that they were standing close to the One Who was greater than Elisha! Jesus, Son of God, was actually Elisha's God! Nothing would ever be impossible for Him! "God" was standing right there and they didn't know it.*

*Do we reason like those men? They thought there's nothing more that can be done. Time to give up hope for a miracle and try to make the best of it. Instead of thinking in the natural realm only, let's believe what the Bible says, "With men this is impossible, but with God all things are possible." (Matthew 19:26).*

*When we put our eyes only on our circumstances, it opens the door to fear. Fear causes us to give up on God or to trust in something man can do. Keep our eyes on Jesus, trusting in what He will do! Jesus is the Author and Finisher of our faith. He is the Originator and the Perfecter of our faith. (Hebrews 12:2). If we are willing, He will help us keep our eyes on Him.*

*This part of the story speaks about life's interruptions. Interruptions do not phase Jesus! I want to be like Jesus and be steady and patient when things are out of my control. I believe Jesus will always be with me and help me.*

\* \* \* \* \* \* \*

Jesus refused to listen to the devastating news the messengers brought. He told Jairus, "Don't be afraid. All you have to do is keep on believing." Jairus did not discuss anything with Jesus. We get the impression from the text that he did not say another word during their walk to his house. He was totally leaning on Jesus, trusting Him. He may have been thinking negative thoughts, but he did not speak them out. He chose to be quiet and trust.

## Selah . . . Pause and Reflect

*Can you imagine what Jairus must have felt in his body when he heard the news that his daughter had died? He was human, like we are...stomach in a knot, a feeling of weakness. All he could do is keep repeating in his mind the words of Jesus, "Guard against fear, it wants to take over. Keep on believing in Me." That walk must have seemed much longer than usual right then.*

*Heart Check: How would you have felt if you heard similar news? Most of us have experienced something upsetting - divorce papers, a doctor's report, an accident with injuries, a friend or spouse who died and other significant traumas. The answer is always the same. Keep our eyes on Jesus, trust Him.*

\* \* \* \* \* \*

Jesus took Peter, James and John with Him to Jairus' house. When they arrived, they were greeted with those who were weeping and wailing. It seems that the family of Jairus did not have the faith in Jesus that he had. Not expecting a miracle, they got the customary funeral proceedings started. Jesus told the mourners - "Why all this weeping? Don't you know this girl is not dead, but merely sleeping?"

They responded by ridiculing Him. (Not a good idea!) He simply ordered them to leave. Then He took the girl's father and mother and His three disciples and went into the room where the girl was lying. Jesus gently took her hand and said, "Little girl, wake up." She immediately rose up and walked!

## *Selah . . . Pause and Reflect*

*When she came back to life and walked around the room, everyone was overcome with joy to see this miracle! Jesus gave practical advice; He had them bring something for her to eat.*

*Jesus cautioned them to not speak about this miracle. Perhaps just let people think the girl was not actually dead. That's what the skeptics would be saying anyway.*

*Heart Check: It would be unlikely the parents could keep this miracle from being talked about. They could, however, refuse to disclose anything that was said or done by Jesus in the privacy of the girl's bedroom. They could also choose to avoid answering direct questions by replying, "Well, what do you think?" Then say nothing in response to what they say. Actually, I really have no good answer on how they would be able to keep quiet about this miracle! I'm just guessing!! What do you think?*

\* \* \* \* \* \*

*WHO IS JESUS FOR US TODAY?*

*Jesus gives us ABUNDANT LIFE!*

*He is LIFE Himself and He lives in us.*

\* \* \* \* \* \*

## WHAT DID WE LEARN FROM THIS STORY?

*Jesus proved that He loved people by putting
their needs above His own.*

*Jairus cared deeply for his daughter. Love made him
determined to find Jesus to heal her.*

*Trust in the Lord's Goodness, Love and Power!
He wants to help us with everything!*

*Jairus had two "interruptions" to deal with.
First, the woman delayed their journey and then
the news of his daughter's death. How
do we deal with interruptions? We can think faith or
we can think fear. (2 Timothy 1:7).*

*When Jairus was told that his daughter died, Jesus said to him,
"That's not the end of the story! There are other facts that
are higher than the ones you are hearing!" Fact:
"Nothing is impossible with God!" (Luke 1:37).*

# TWO BLIND MEN

## Matthew 9:27-31

*Matthew 9:27 When Jesus departed from there, two bind men followed Him, crying out and saying, "Son of David, have mercy on us!"*

Isaiah 35:5 talks about a time when, "the eyes of the blind would be opened and the ears of the deaf will be unstopped." Perhaps these men had heard from friends or a Rabbi that miracles for the blind and deaf were believed to happen when the Messiah came. Now these men were hearing about amazing miracles done by Jesus. People were talking! Could this be the Messiah? Many who were healed were convinced that Jesus was the Messiah they had been waiting for.

This story begins as Jesus was returning from the home of Jairus. Two blind men began following Him and shouted out, "Son of David, have mercy on us!" Jesus did not respond and went into a house.

## Selah . . . Pause and Reflect

*The term "Son of David" was a popular term for the Messiah. People in those days saw the Messiah as a military hero or a political figure that would rescue the Jews from their bondage to the Romans.*

*Jesus must have heard these blind men calling to Him for healing. Why did He ignore them and keep on going? He stopped for Bartimaeus, but not for them. I don't know the answer to why He ignored them. Could it be that He wanted to make sure they understood He was not going to rescue Israel at that time? This was the time He came as their Savior and Lord. Could it be because He was testing their faith? Did He want see if they were determined enough to continue to seek Him for their miracle? Did He wonder if they would keep their faith alive, even when they faced an obstacle (like Him ignoring them)?*

*Heart Check: In every situation involving healing, Jesus always did the right thing at the right time. He depended on the Father to let Him know what to do. Jesus did not ignore these two blind men because He was tired and wanted privacy. Most of His ministry was done during long, tiring days. His compassion for each individual was greater than His desire to rest or eat.*

\* \* \* \* \* \* \*

The two blind men just walked right into the house after Jesus! Love those guys! Doesn't that show determination? Being formal and dignified by being invited in was not on their agenda! They were determined! They did not knock or wait to be invited into the house. They could apologize later for their lack of etiquette! They were NOT going to miss this opportunity to see Jesus, the Healer. Too much was at stake. They wanted their miserable lives to be a thing of the past. They saw their chance for a normal life with sight! Jesus was near. He had proven healing powers! "This is our moment," they thought!

## Selah . . . Pause and Reflect

*The life of a blind person was not easy. Every day would be the same. In the morning, they would find their way to the Beggar's Row on the main road through town. People passed by. Some dropped coins in their cup, a few called them outcasts and sarcastically asked: "Was it you or your parents that sinned?" Hhmmmm??*

*<u>Heart Check:</u> When we see people struggling now days, do we stop to think about what their daily life is like? Or, do we pass by, thinking how glad we are just to get away because we don't know what to say? Who knows, if we had the same background and disadvantages, we might be right beside them!*

\* \* \* \* \* \*

Jesus said to the two men, "Do you believe that I am able to do this?" They said to Him, "Yes, Lord." The key word is "Lord!" Jesus must have loved hearing that! It showed their hearts and that they knew exactly Who He was. At this point in time, He wasn't their military or political leader, coming to rescue their nation. He was their Lord. He wasn't just a mere man, He was the Son of Jehovah God! He was Lord!

Then Jesus touched their eyes. For a blind person, touch would be a language they understood. Jesus said, "According to your faith, let it be to you." And their eyes were opened! Wow! The first person's face they saw was of their Savior, their Healer! I'm thinking they stared at Him, as if to burn into their memories that beautiful, amazing Face.

## Selah . . . Pause and Reflect

*They passed the "faith test!" They didn't have to prove to be "good enough" to earn their healing. And, Jesus would not withhold their healing because they were "bad enough." Healing simply came from Jesus because that was the will of the Father for all of His children.*

*The faith test is simply - do we believe that Jesus is willing and able to heal us? When the crowds came and Jesus healed them all, He didn't interview them first to find out if they qualified. He only wanted them to believe in Him. To believe that He would do what He says He will do. He is our Healer!*

*Heart Check: The Old Testament and New Testament are full of examples of how the sick were healed. Nothing is impossible when we trust in the Lord! The two blind men were determined! We can be too. We can cast our cares on Him, because He cares for us. (1 Peter 5:7).*

\* \* \* \* \* \* \*

Jesus gave them a stern warning not to not tell anyone about their healing. Why did He say that when He told the demoniac to go and tell everyone? These two instances were done in different geographical regions. The demon possessed man was on the east side of the Sea of Galilee. Jesus knew the man's deliverance would be a strong testimony to his family and others in those ten towns of The Decapolis. There would be no chance of large mobs since Jesus was not coming back to that area. He went there only once.

## Selah . . . Pause and Reflect

*The west side of the Sea of Galilee contained the towns that Jesus had ministered in for many months, especially in and around Capernaum. The large crowds that followed Him provoked the Pharisees to want to stop such "heresy" being taught by this rogue Teacher. There were times when they got together to plot His death.*

*Jesus knew exactly when His time to die would be, and He did not want to deviate from that holy plan. Could that be the reason He told the two men not to spread the news about healing? He knew when the confrontation should and would come with the ruling religious class. He still had some months of ministry ahead of Him.*

*Heart Check: Think about it. How hard would it be for those two formerly blind men to keep quiet about receiving their sight?! Anyone who knew them as beggars alongside the road would know that they certainly are not going back to doing that now that they could see! The miracle would be obvious to anyone just by observing them.*

*Perhaps at first they tried to keep things quiet, but once news got out, it would be hard to deny the facts. News spreads fast! Jesus always wants us to obey Him. Could they just disappear into a different town where no one knew them? That's probably not do-able, since they would not have the resources as former beggars. It was a dilemma. What would you do?*

\* \* \* \* \* \*

*WHO IS JESUS FOR US TODAY?*

*Jesus rewarded their FAITH and DETERMINATION.*

*He is pleased when we confidently press in for healing.*

\* \* \* \* \* \*

*WHAT DID WE LEARN FROM THIS STORY?*

*These men believed Jesus came from God, He
was the long-awaited Messiah.*

*We believe that healing is for us and we will continue
to expect it until it is manifested in our body.*

*We will not give up! Jesus helps us to believe.*

*The focus of our faith is always on Jesus and what
He did. His will is for us to be healed.*

*Jesus is the Author and Finisher of our faith, the
Originator and the Perfecter of our faith.
(Hebrews 12:2).*

# TWO MUTE MEN
# WITH DEMONS

Matthew 9:32-33      Matthew 12:22

*Matthew 9:32-33 As they went out, behold, they brought to Him a man, mute and demon-possessed. And when the demon was cast out, the mute spoke. And the multitudes marveled, saying, "It was never seen like this in Israel!"*

*Matthew 12:22 Then one was brought to Him who was demon-possessed, blind and mute; and He healed him, so that the blind and mute man both spoke and saw.*

Matthew wrote about two different men in two different time frames. One was blind, the other one was not. They were both possessed by a demon and neither one could speak.

## Selah . . . Pause and Reflect

Both of *these men were brought into the Presence of Jesus, Who has total power over all of Satan's works. Matthew 9:33 says that when the demon was cast out, the mute spoke. That indicates that the demon was the cause of why that man could not speak.*

*Matthew 12:22 says that Jesus "healed him, so that the blind and mute man both spoke and saw." Then in v24 the Pharisees wanted to discredit the source of Jesus' authority. They said that He cast out demons by the power of Beelzebub, the prince of demons. The Pharisees acknowledged that getting rid of the demon was what produced the healing this man needed.*

*Heart Check: Jesus has imparted to us His authority to overcome every power that Satan possesses. Nothing will harm us when we walk in the authority Jesus has given us. (Luke 10:19). Let's stay close to Jesus.*

\* \* \* \* \* \* \*

Matthew tells us in 12:22 that this man was blind and could not speak. He could hear, and that would have been somewhat beneficial. However, how would he communicate a response to what he heard? Being blind he would not be able to write his thoughts out. His situation must have been frustrating for him and everyone around him. Can you picture what life would be like for him? We need all three parts to work - sight, hearing and speech!

## *Selah . . . Pause and Reflect*

*Most of us know people who have some kind of limitation. Granted, not as life-changing as these men's limitations were. Some are living with pain or disease and the restrictions those things bring. Some live with the trauma of the death of someone close, a failed marriage, rebellious children and more.*

*Heart Check: How does the Lord want us to respond to people in pain? We have Jesus living in us, so we can respond like*

*He would. We can use the same compassion Jesus has and pray for any situation to be resolved by the power of the Lord.*

\* \* \* \* \* \*

Matthew does not include details for either one of these healings. These miracles are recorded in Matthew using one verse (12:22) and two verses (9:32-33)! The men were brought to Jesus, and He healed and delivered them! Yay! What a change that would be for them! Now they each had a LIFE!!! Also a big change for their families and friends to be able to communicate with them.

## Selah . . . Pause and Reflect

*Jesus always responds to faith. Both of these men were brought to Jesus by others. The ones who brought them had most likely seen Jesus heal someone or heard stories about Him. Their faith in Jesus to heal was based on what they knew about Him. Isn't it the same for us?*

*Heart Check: Can you picture HOPE rising in the hearts of the ones who brought each of these men to Jesus? "If this Man of God gave deliverance and healing to others, surely He will heal our man as well!" And, He did, for both of them!*

\* \* \* \* \* \*

Jesus represented the character of Father God perfectly. When He was on earth, He did what He saw in His mind and heart what the Father would do. We're told in Lamentations 3:22 that the Father's heart is full of mercy and compassion. Jesus also showed that compassion toward anyone who came to Him with a problem. These men were no exception.

## Selah . . . Pause and Reflect

*Jesus had a way of tuning out all distractions and giving His complete focus to the person who stood in front of Him. His care and compassion could be seen by looking into those eyes filled with love and seeing the welcoming smile on His face.*

*<u>Heart Check:</u> What would it feel like to stand before Jesus? Could you sense His delight in YOU and how much He wants YOU to have the best life ever?!*

\* \* \* \* \* \* \*

### WHO IS JESUS FOR US TODAY?

*The heart of Jesus is full of MERCY and COMPASSION!*

*He wants the best life for all of us!*

\* \* \* \* \* \* \*

### WHAT DID WE LEARN FROM THIS STORY?

*One verse or two verses! Simple!*
*Brought to Jesus and healed!*

*Serious problems? Not for Jesus!*

*Jesus demonstrated Compassion, we can too!*

*What Jesus has done for others, He'll do for us!*

*Jesus is delighted with us! He wants to bless us!*

*When we look at Jesus we will see The Father's heart.*

# FEEDING OF THE 5,000

Matthew 14:12-21      Mark 6:30-44

Luke 9:10-17      John 6:1-14

*Mark 6:31-32 Jesus said to His disciples, "Come aside by yourselves to a deserted place and rest awhile"...so they departed to a deserted place in the boat by themselves.*

The disciples were returning from their two-by-two journeys to preach the Kingdom of God and heal the sick. They had stories to tell Jesus about all they had done and taught. A peaceful rest and refreshing was needed for all.

They arrived on the other side of the lake and it wasn't long before a great crowd made their way to find Jesus. His heart was deeply moved with compassion toward them. He said they were like sheep without a shepherd.

The compassion of Jesus prompted Him to heal anyone that needed healing. He also taught them, speaking about the Kingdom of God.

## Selah . . . Pause and Reflect

*Picture yourself in that crowd. You and a friend are sitting close enough to Jesus that you can sense His love and concern for each person. It's like He knew everyone's name and their story. His heart longed for them to be truly free from the bondage that sin had brought upon the human race.*

*We saw the great delight on His face when someone was set free from a lingering disease. Most of us were here because we had seen or heard of miracles He did. We knew that if we had a need, He would make it right! That was our hope. We were not disappointed.*

*We heard the passion in His voice when He talked about His Father and the ways of the Kingdom. It felt so good to be with Him. Just to be sitting in His presence brought peace.*

*Heart Check: Do we make time to "just be with Jesus?" In our busy lives, it is hard to do sometimes. What motivated those many people to walk up a hill in a deserted place to see Jesus?*

\* \* \* \* \* \* \*

John 6:1-7 records an interesting dialogue between Jesus and Philip. Jesus was aware of people becoming hungry as the day wore on. He asked Philip to tell Him where they could buy bread for the people to eat. Philip answered that 200 denarii worth of bread would not even be enough money for each one to have a little food.

Jesus asked Philip a WHERE question and Philip answered Him with a HOW answer. Two hundred denarii was worth about eight month's wages for the average person. Philip was commenting that it would cost more than that for each person to have just a snack.

Philip's faith was being tested. Jesus wanted to know if Philip would look to Him alone to supply the need and not consider their limited resources. Jesus used this situation to teach Philip a faith lesson.

## Selah . . . Pause and Reflect

*Jesus was interested in building Philip's faith. He was training him to not make the circumstances his focus, but to look to Jesus alone for miracles, wisdom, and everything else that is needed.*

*The next time - and there would be many next times - Jesus and the disciples faced an impossible situation, I think Philip was the first to say, "Jesus, I don't know 'the how' this will change for the better, but I believe 'YOU are the HOW' to meet the need!"*

*Heart Check: Philip's lesson from this conversation is also directed toward you and me, 2000 years later. We can boldly say, "Jesus, You are the How in our lives. We will not make our problems bigger than You!"*

\* \* \* \* \* \* \*

The disciples came to Jesus and advised Him that it was time to send this multitude away so they could go somewhere to buy food before dark. There surely was no food in this desolate place! Anyone could see that.

Sometimes the disciples felt they could help Jesus out. This was one of those times. Perhaps Peter led the group; he was a born leader and could easily see a solution to most problems. Peter knew that he and his friends were capable of giving orders and for being heard! They could disperse this crowd in no time! This is an example of our human nature to "try works" rather than to "trust Jesus."

## Selah . . . Pause and Reflect

*Jesus was teaching His followers to surrender their own ideas and plans and be open to His ways. He is teaching us the same thing. Our Bible is full of God's truth and wisdom. We gain His way of thinking by pondering the Scriptures. When we have surrendered our will to His, we know the outcome will be good and beneficial. We have peace when we are on the right track.*

*Heart Check: Are we looking at things the same as Jesus does? He always has good for us. He wants us to cooperate with Him regarding the destiny He has planned for us. We all have a purpose to fulfill in this life. Are we on board with His plan? Is there "more" ahead for us that we need to talk to God about?*

\* \* \* \* \* \* \*

Jesus simply answered, "You give them something to eat!"

Use your imagination to see the faces of those twelve men at that moment. They were most likely staring at Jesus, thinking "What did He just say?!" There was a very large crowd of hungry families and not a store in sight to buy food for them!

Andrew said to Jesus, "There is a boy here who has five barley loaves and two small fish, What are they among so many?" Jesus didn't even acknowledge Andrew's disclaimer about the ridiculousness of such a small amount.

Jesus simply thanked the lad, took his lunch, smiled and gave him a hug. The boy willingly gave his lunch to Jesus and gained the precious experience of a smile and a hug from the Savior of the World. The events of that day must have stayed in the boy's mind and heart for a long time. Perhaps he went to bed that night with a smile on his face. He had seen HIS lunch multiplied to feed everyone! Wow. He was already thinking that he had the best ever Show and Tell Story for his class at school!

## Selah . . . Pause and Reflect

*Has the Lord ever asked you to do something you thought was too big? (You feed them!) The young boy didn't try to figure it out, he only wanted to help. He just gave what he had. We tend to think we are "not good enough" and we hold back. We compare with others and find fault in ourselves. Let's be like the lad who just let Jesus decide about "good enough." The Bible tells us that there were 5,000 men. The women and children were not counted. The "boy whose lunch didn't count" was the one to make the miracle happen!*

*<u>Heart check:</u> Think about those seemingly "impossible things" as being a way to see God's enabling power flow to you and through you. We benefit when we believe for and expect God's miracle working power in any area of our life. Instead of a lunch, we can give Jesus our trust, our obedience and our worship. That results in His power flowing through us to enable us.*

\* \* \* \* \* \* \*

The disciples expressed what they thought was a good plan: send the people away! Jesus did not rebuke them for that. He simply modeled for them a better way. A faith way. He was demonstrating His trust in the Father to take care of ALL the needs of the people.

Jesus knew the love and care the Father had for each person in the crowd because He, Himself had that same love for everyone. Jesus also knew there were no impossible situations in God's realm, only opportunities. Jesus looked at life through the eyes of trust in His Father. Anything the Father wanted done would be totally do-able!

## Selah . . . Pause and Reflect

*The disciples were looking at the situation through natural eyes, not spiritual eyes. We are born with senses that tell us what is going on. We see, we hear, we feel, we touch and smell. The disciples were trying to come up with the best solution using their natural senses. They were not thinking that Jesus might have an alternative way, a spiritual way, of handling things.*

*Heart Check: Do you and I see "impossible situations" or "opportunities?" It takes a mind renewed with the Word to turn a negative situation into something that we let God take care of. It's all about the lens we view situations with. It takes a determination to see and do things God's way.*

\* \* \* \* \* \* \*

Jesus wanted things to be orderly. He knew exactly what He was planning to do. He called for the disciples to have the people sit down in groups of fifty. Then there would be grassy pathways for the twelve to walk on.

When the guys were finished arranging the crowd, Jesus took the five loaves and two fish and looked up to heaven. Jesus blessed and broke the five loaves and two fish. The miracle of multiplication began with the Giving of Thanks. Then He gave the fish and bread to His disciples to distribute. Each one saw the food become enough as they passed it out!

Everyone ate as much as they wanted. They were fully satisfied; no one was left out. Philip dared to hope that everyone would have just a small amount. Andrew mentioned the little they did have was surely not enough. At the end of the day, everyone saw that more than enough food had been passed out! Each disciple took away a basket of leftovers!

## Selah . . . Pause and Reflect

*Does our little make a difference? Did that boy's small lunch make a difference? Did Jesus need food, even just a little food, to be able to multiply it? Evidently He did. Actually, food multiplied when the disciples handed it out.*

*How do we see ourselves? At first, Philip, Andrew and the others did not see themselves as part of a Jesus Team to bring dinner to all those people. Jesus wants us to be His hands and feet. Help us to be willing, Lord! It's not Jesus alone and it's not us alone, it's both Jesus and us.*

*<u>Heart Check:</u> Do you have a "little" you can give to the Master? Can He make our small offering become something special in someone's life? A good word, a kind deed to make someone's day!*

\* \* \* \* \* \*

Jesus kept amazing the disciples with how He triumphed over every obstacle! When they didn't have any idea of what was coming next, Jesus showed them something new and wonderful about Himself! They expressed their profound gratitude for the ability to do life with the Son of God!

## Selah . . . Pause and Reflect

*It helps to see Jesus as our constant companion. He will never leave us. What we think and say about a situation is where our faith is. Let's introduce a new word into our daily vocabulary - Opportunity!*

*Heart Check: Jesus wants to live His life through each one of us. It's up to us to let Him do that. He doesn't remind us of our faults and failings. That would be the job of "the accuser." Jesus is the One who whispers, "You can do this! I will be with you to help you!"*

*Thank You Jesus, for choosing us, for loving us and thinking the best of us! We're so grateful we get to do life with the Son of God!*

\* \* \* \* \* \* \*

*WHO IS JESUS FOR US TODAY?*

*Jesus is the GOD of the IMPOSSIBLE!*

*He turned a problem into an opportunity.*

\* \* \* \* \* \* \*

## WHAT DID WE LEARN FROM THIS STORY?

*We make being in the Presence of Jesus a priority.*

*Why would we climb a hillside to get near to Jesus?*
*What are we looking for, what are we hungry for?*

*Jesus will always be our HOW. He is enough.*

*We don't try to fix things ourselves, we look to Jesus.*

*Jesus wants us to give Him "our little."*

*We are on The Jesus Team! We are His hands*
*and feet. We can't help but win!*

# CANAANITE WOMAN'S DAUGHTER

Mathew 15:21-28     Mark 7:24-30

*Matthew 15:21-23 Then Jesus went out from there and departed to the region of Tyre and Sidon. And behold, a woman of Canaan came from that region and cried out to Him, saying, "Have mercy on me, O Lord, Son of David! My daughter is severely demon-possessed." But He answered her not a word. And His disciples came and urged Him, saying, "Send her away, for she cries out after us."*

Traveling north from Capernaum, Jesus arrived in the Gentile territory of Tyre and Sidon, located in modern day Lebanon on the Mediterranean coast. Mark tells us that Jesus intended to slip into a house unnoticed. When a woman whose daughter had a demon spirit heard He was there, she came and threw herself down at His feet. She was a Syro-Phoenician by birth, and she kept asking Him to cast the demon out of her daughter.

## Selah . . . Pause and Reflect

*This desperate mother was very determined to get a miracle for her daughter who was suffering under the influence of a demon. She told Jesus that her daughter was "severely demon-possessed." That sounds like the daughter and also her mother had a really difficult life! Can you imagine?*

*"Send her away! She is bothering us!" Compassion was not their strong point! This is not the first time the disciples gave Jesus some practical advice! It just shows how we, as*

*humans, are so tuned into the natural. Jesus always had His antenna up to tune into the supernatural realm of His Father. Everything He did and said was wrapped in pure and powerful Love!*

<u>*Heart Check:*</u> *Notice the boldness of this woman, even after the annoyed disciples made a fuss and wanted her gone. Even after Jesus Himself did not answer her. Ouch! That's a tough one! She still didn't give up! What would we have done at that point?*

*She knew she had no rights! She was not included in God's covenant with His people. She had no promise to claim as a Gentile. Yet, she trusted completely in the compassion of Jesus and kept on with her petition for a miracle. Amazing.*

\* \* \* \* \* \*

Jesus told her that He was only sent to those in the house of Israel. He also pointed out that "it is not good to take the children's bread and throw it to the little dogs."

## *Selah . . . Pause and Reflect*

*The children's bread referred to healing and other blessings Jesus brought first to the Children of Israel. After He was raised from the dead, the book of Acts tells us that the gospel spread to other nations with signs and wonders.*

*Jews called the Gentiles "dogs" and they meant the wild dogs that fed on garbage. It was an insulting term. Jesus softened the word to indicate a house pet, like the family puppy.*

*Heart Check:* Faith comes by hearing the good news about Jesus. Someone, somewhere, must have told this woman about Jesus and the miracles He had done. Her faith was reacting to what she had heard about Him. This was the only time Jesus left Jewish territory. Was she the reason He went there?

\* \* \* \* \* \*

She answered Him, saying that even the little dogs under the table eat the children's crumbs.

## Selah . . . Pause and Reflect

*She wasn't too proud to identify herself as a little dog! She didn't want to take anything away from "the children." She thought, "Let them have all the bread healing and blessing they want and more! I only need a crumb and I'm happy." She knew she was not worthy of His blessing and there was no way she could earn a blessing.*

*Heart Check: In her heart, she must have come to the conclusion that Jesus not only possessed power to help people, but that He overflowed with love for individual people. She wanted to tap into that love that was greater than any rules! Perhaps, the stories she heard about Jesus healing everyone and caring so much for each person, made her trust that His compassionate heart alone would override all barriers of culture.*

\* \* \* \* \* \*

Jesus said to her, "Oh woman, great is your faith." She turned those obstacles into stepping stones.

## Selah . . . Pause and Reflect

*This precious woman lived with a difficult situation! She daily dealt with issues with her daughter that most all of us know nothing about. Jesus knew. He always knew the history of the ones He prayed for. The Spirit within Him would give Him supernatural knowledge. I believe tremendous compassion rose up within Him toward this woman and her daughter.*

*Heart Check: This situation revealed to us that not everyone or every need had to fit into a certain "box." For Jesus to bring deliverance and healing to this girl was not the kosher thing to do because she and her mother were not part of the Children of Israel that Jesus was sent to minister to.*

\* \* \* \* \* \*

Jesus told this woman, "What you desire will be done for you." And at that very moment, her daughter was instantly set free from demonic torment.

## Selah . . . Pause and Reflect

*What do you think caused Jesus to respond to her and give her what she asked for? Was it because she was a desperate woman, seeking help for the daughter that she loved? We can relate when we pray earnestly for someone we love that needs a supernatural touch from God. Love is powerful! It bears all things, believes all things, hopes all things, endures all things. Love never fails! (1 Corinthians 13:7-8a).*

*Was it her persistence? Jesus explained that concept in the story about the unjust judge. Luke 18:7 says, "And shall God not avenge (vindicate) His own elect who cry out day and night to Him, though He bears long with them?"*

*Heart Check: Was it her humility that touched the heart of Jesus? The Lord promises that the humble will be lifted up. Peter reminds us that God resists the proud, but gives grace to the humble. "Therefore, humble yourselves under the mighty hand of God, that He may exalt you in due time, casting all your care upon Him, for He cares for you." (1 Peter 5:5b-7). There is a comma after the words "in due time." Isn't it interesting that a humble person will give their cares to God, while by implication, a proud person would not think to do that. Hhmmm...*

\* \* \* \* \* \* \*

On this occasion Jesus did not go to the girl to liberate her from demons. Every other occasion recorded of deliverances, Jesus was with the person involved. We are told in Matthew 15:28 that the girl was set free the very hour her mother was talking to Jesus.

What does that show us? It proves that the words of Jesus are full of power to heal and deliver, even at a distance. John 6:63 tells us the words of Jesus are "Spirit, and they are Life!"

What if Jesus recognized this woman's genuine faith in Him? What if He wanted to draw it out of her even further? She had to overcome human barriers, one by one. Let's list what she encountered:

- The silence of Jesus. It's hard for us to keep on praying to God when He seems to be ignoring us, not listening to our prayers. When Jesus didn't immediately respond to her, she refused to quit in her pursuit of a miracle. She persevered with patience.
- The disciples begged Jesus to send her away. The disciples lacked sympathy for her problem. Could this callous response by all these men be discouraging? Sure! Discouraging, and also she could've taken offense and left in a huff. But she chose not to listen to what the disciples said. She wasn't there to talk to them anyway!
- She was a Gentile and had no claim on Jesus. Jesus said He was sent to the lost sheep of the house of Israel. Her answer was to worship Him saying, "Lord, help me." She called Him Lord. She was appealing for His mercy and grace.
- Then there was the seeming insult from Jesus! After being referred to as a little dog, she could have turned around and slowly walked away. She chose to answer Jesus in a humble way and be grateful for the crumbs! Her faith stayed strong, she was determined.

She overcame all four obstacles! She was like Jacob, who wrestled with God. She deserved the commendation of Jesus - "Great is your faith!" She was one of only two people recorded in the Bible that Jesus praised for having strong faith. The other one was the centurion.

\* \* \* \* \* \*

## *WHO IS JESUS FOR US TODAY?*

*Jesus is the REWARDER of our PERSISTENT FAITH.*

*He is the answer to anything that seems impossible.*

*\* \* \* \* \* \* \**

## *WHAT DID WE LEARN FROM THIS STORY?*

*The woman cried out, "Have mercy on me, O Lord, Son of David!" "The Lord is gracious and full of compassion, slow to anger and great in mercy." Psalm 145:8 We can always expect mercy from Jesus.*

*Jesus intended to slip into a house unnoticed. Instead, He allowed this woman to capture His heart. He does the same with us. He's never too busy for us!*

*Are we tuned in to "the natural" like the disciples, or tuned in to "the Spirit" like Jesus?*

*She believed that Jesus overflowed with love for individual people. Do we believe that?*

*She had no promise to claim as a Gentile. We have many promises to claim as Children of God!*

*She passed the four human barriers test. How would we do with those four?*

# DEAF MAN WITH SPEECH DEFECT

## Mark 7:31-37

*Mark 7:32 They brought to Him one who was deaf and had an impediment in his speech, and they begged Him to put His hand on him.*

This miracle took place on the east side of the Sea of Galilee as Jesus was coming back from Tyre and Sidon. A deaf man was brought to Jesus who could not speak plainly. Those that brought the man pleaded with Him to lay hands on him and heal him.

It's interesting to note that Jesus did not do what they asked Him to do. He did not place His hand on the man. Jesus seldom did the same thing when He healed people. He depended on the Father for directions in all situations. Everything He did fit perfectly with the person receiving the healing.

## Selah . . . Pause and Reflect

*Think about how frustrating it would be to not be able to hear! For this man, daily life went by in total silence while he could see others talking and laughing. He wondered what they were laughing about. He wished he could be laughing with them. He could have felt left out and alone.*

*This man was blessed because he had people who cared for him. Perhaps they were his family, we don't know. At any rate, they brought him to Jesus. They had possibly heard beforehand of Jesus opening deaf ears.*

*Heart Check: Someone who lives with a deaf person can be almost as distressed as the one whose hearing has failed. Before sign language, how would anyone find out what the deaf person is thinking, how they are feeling or what they want? Deafness for this man would affect those living around him, as well as himself.*

*Jesus understood the situations involved in this man's life. Joy would bubble up in Him, just because He knew how many people would be glad when this man was able to hear and speak again! Just imagine the late night story-telling sessions when the family would answer his questions about this person and that occasion. They would also hear him share what he felt and thought in times past. It would be wonderful for him to really get to know his family and for them to get to know him.*

\* \* \* \* \* \* \*

Jesus took the man away from the crowd to a private spot. Perhaps He sensed the man would be more comfortable where he wouldn't be the focus of attention for an excited crowd. Jesus was sensitive to how each person would best receive ministry.

This man could not hear Jesus tell him what was going to happen next. So, Jesus demonstrated to him the ministry He was about to perform by putting His fingers in the man's ears. Jesus communicated with the man using the language of touch.

Then Jesus placed some of His saliva on the man's tongue. Saliva was thought to have healing properties in those days. The saliva from Jesus would have represented "life" because Jesus possessed life in Himself.

## *Selah . . . Pause and Reflect*

*The kind and thoughtful heart of Jesus wanted to let this man know what was coming next. Wouldn't that bless and encourage the man to feel the touch of Jesus' fingers in his ears? He got the message! There's going to be a change in those deaf ears! Yay!*

*In the past, when he tried to speak, people would look at him with a quizzical glance. He knew they did not understand his garbled speech. This was very frustrating for him and the ones he wanted to communicate with.*

*For him to receive the saliva of Jesus was another sign that Jesus was doing a thorough job of making him normal like everyone else! It could be that he could not speak plainly because of his hearing loss. Even before Jesus actually spoke "Be opened," the man knew that he would be healed. Jesus helped to develop his faith by the things He did.*

*Heart Check: Jesus tunes into our needs. He doesn't expect us to know everything about spiritual things. He treats us the same as the deaf man. He teaches us in ways we can understand and grasp. He is not here physically to touch our ears or put saliva on our tongue, but He brings Bible verses, sermons, friends and books; all ways for us to hear His voice.*

\* \* \* \* \* \* \*

Jesus looked up to heaven, He sighed deeply, and spoke to the man's ears and tongue: "Be opened!" Immediately, his ears were opened, his tongue was loosed, and he spoke plainly. What a happy day for this man and his family!

Jesus ordered everyone to keep this miracle a secret and tell no one. The more He told them not to, the more the news spread! Jesus had reasons for everything He did and said.

## Selah . . . Pause and Reflect

*The crowd was astonished beyond measure at this miracle! They began to declare, "He has done all things well! He even makes the deaf to hear and the mute speak!" In days past, a person could live their whole life and never see that happen, or even think it could happen. The healing power that Jesus carried amazed them all.*

*Heart Check: We don't have Jesus walking the earth in person right now. If we have ever asked Him to be our Savior, He came to live in our heart by His Spirit. He really is with us. Jesus still does all things well today!*

\* \* \* \* \* \*

### WHO IS JESUS FOR US TODAY?

*Jesus is our GAME CHANGER! Nothing is too hard for Him.*

*He makes bad things good with just one touch.*

\* \* \* \* \* \*

*WHAT DID WE LEARN FROM THIS STORY?*

*We can be a friend to someone and bring them to Jesus.*

*Don't expect Jesus to always do things the same way.*

*What do we want to see "Open Up!" in our life?*

# BLIND MAN IN BETHSAIDA

## Mark 8:22-26

*Matthew 8:22 Then He came to Bethsaida; and they brought a blind man to Him, and begged Him to touch him.*

Bethsaida was a prosperous city, a fishing port on the shores of the Sea of Galilee. Jesus spoke a rebuke in Matthew 11:21 - "Woe to you Bethsaida! For if the mighty works which were done in you had been done in Tyre and Sidon, they would have repented long ago in sackcloth and ashes."

The people in this prosperous city found no need for faith in the gospel or repentance. When we have everything we want, plus a lot more, typically, we don't need God. Does that sound familiar for us today?

Mark is the only one of the gospel writers to record this story. It must have made an impression on him. This account is different from other blind men who received their sight. This man did not come to Jesus on his own, he was brought by others who begged Jesus to heal him.

## Selah . . . Pause and Reflect

*We learn from the rest of the story that this man could identify a man and a tree and the difference between them. He could have had his sight at one time and lost it through injury or disease. Have you ever lost something? Like the ability to walk? Any loss could be devastating. It would be easy to*

*be discouraged and loose all hope of being normal again,
especially as time went on and there was no improvement.*

*<u>Heart Check:</u> This man had friends who "hoped" for him!
They were his link to the only One who could make things
right. At that moment, they believed for him and spoke to
Jesus for him. We can do that as well.*

\* \* \* \* \* \*

Jesus guided the man out of the town. And when He had spit on his
eyes and put His hands on him, He asked him if he saw anything.

When we think of "spitting" on someone, we are used to the
negative connotation of derision. Indeed, Jesus received the
insulting action of being spit on during the beatings after His
arrest. However, even "the cross" shows us how Jesus turned a
cursed thing into a most blessed thing. Anything that came from
the body of Jesus would be anointed and powerful. For the man
to feel that show of such a personal ministry must have had a
deep impact on him. Jesus also put His hands on the man's eyes.
Touch was the language of a blind person. He couldn't see the
love coming from the face of Jesus, but he could feel the comfort
of what he knew to be healing touches.

## *Selah . . . Pause and Reflect*

*Jesus treated each person differently. He respected them as
unique individuals. Jesus depended on the Father to reveal
the personality and needs of each person and to guide Him
in the best way to minister life to them. Jesus took the man by
the hand and led him out of the town. He knew the crowd
would have been a distraction for this man.*

*Heart Check: Jesus deeply cares for each one of us! He knows us better than we know ourselves! He wants to help each one of us to live a life of blessing and freedom. NO ONE is excluded from His loving care! HE is our Hope!*

\* \* \* \* \* \* \*

The man told Jesus that his sight was coming back and that he could see men, but they looked like walking trees! The second time Jesus put His hands on the man's eyes, his sight was fully restored and he could see clearly. What JOY for him to see the beautiful face of his Lord Jesus first!!

## Selah . . . Pause and Reflect

*The Bible doesn't tell us that Jesus prayed for the man's eyes to be opened. He didn't speak the words, "Be healed." He knew that healing would flow through His hands, so He put His hands on the man's eyes twice.*

*Jesus spoke to the man each time after he took His hands off. The first time, He asked him if he saw anything. The second time He made the man look up. Isn't it interesting that Jesus did not go by a formula when He healed someone? Each one had a personal experience with the Lord Jesus.*

*Heart Check: How should we react when we are expecting something to happen in a certain way and it doesn't happen that way? We keep trusting, keep hoping and keep expecting the Lord to be good to those who wait for Him. This healing is unique in that it was accomplished in stages.*

\* \* \* \* \* \* \*

Jesus sent the man back to his home with these instructions, "Don't go into the town and don't tell anyone in the town about your healing." Basically, He told this man (and others He healed), that there was a right time for everything and they would do well to "wait for that right time." Did they do what He said? Not so much. Do we like to wait? Not so much.

## Selah . . . Pause and Reflect

*Why would Jesus tell people to keep such good news quiet? Maybe it was because He knew the exact time for the crucifixion and it was not to take place for another whole year, in the Spring of A.D. 30. Jesus had many more towns and villages to reach before His work was done. He knew the religious community was already agitated over this "false prophet" named Jesus. He did not want to be arrested before His time.*

*Heart Check: There are many verses in the Bible that talk about "waiting." Lamentations 3:25 says, "The Lord is good to those who wait for Him, to the soul that seeks Him." Our part is to seek Him, His part is to be good to us!*

\* \* \* \* \* \*

### WHO IS JESUS FOR US TODAY?

*Jesus is a patient HEALER, He won't quit until it is done.*

*He wants each of us to experience abundant life!*

\* \* \* \* \* \*

## WHAT DID WE LEARN FROM THIS STORY?

*This man did not come to Jesus on his own. He was brought
by others who begged Jesus to heal him.*

*At first, his friends had the hope and the faith for him.
This healing was gradual. Jesus put His hands on him twice.*

*Jesus led the man out of the town. Did the town
represent "unbelief?" (Matthew 11:21)*

*Jesus ministered to him with a loving touch, which
would have encouraged his faith.*

*Knowing that we are totally and completely loved helps
faith to be strong in us to receive from God.*

# BOY WITH DEMON

## Matthew 17:14-21     Mark 9:14-29     Luke 9:37-42

*Mark 9:14 And when He came to the disciples, He saw a great multitude around them, and scribes disputing with them.*

When Jesus and the three disciples came down from the Mount of Transfiguration, they encountered a large crowd. A group of scribes were arguing with the nine disciples as the growing crowd circled around them. Jesus wanted to know what the discussion was about. He knew the scribes would be eager to point out their own interpretation of this situation.

A man from the crowd came to Jesus and let Him know that he was the reason for the confusion. He called Jesus "Teacher," and told Him he had a son who was possessed by a demon that made him unable to speak. He said that he had previously begged the disciples to drive the demon out, but they could not.

## Selah . . . Pause and Reflect

*The boy's father had heard about the miracles Jesus could do and he hoped His disciples could do the same. They failed. He was disappointed. Now, he wasn't sure if Jesus could help in this situation. Maybe the demon had been tormenting the boy too long, making casting it out too difficult. This father had become discouraged. Failure made him open to doubts.*

*This desperate father told Jesus that his son was an only child, and that he was severely tormented. He recounted that when a spirit seized him, he would suddenly cry out. The spirit put the boy into convulsions and departed from him with great difficulty, badly bruising him.*

Heart Check: *Try to imagine what a difficult situation this boy and his parents were in. For mom and dad there would be no rest or time away from their son. They must always be watchful and alert. His parents felt helpless and at times traumatized by what their precious son went through. What a tragic way to live!*

\* \* \* \* \* \* \*

Jesus looked at the crowd and said, "O faithless generation, how long shall I bear with you, bring him to Me." They brought the boy and when the demon saw Jesus, he threw the boy into violent convulsions. He fell to the ground, rolling around and foaming at the mouth.

## Selah . . . Pause and Reflect

*It was not the normal practice of Jesus to publicly correct His disciples. He would teach and train them in private. Jesus used the word "generation," which may have meant he was addressing the crowd, and especially the scribes.*

Heart Check: *Faith is simply believing what is written in the Word of God. It is easy for doubt to come when we keep our focus on the symptoms. Take a look at what Jesus paid for at the whipping post. (1 Peter 2:24).*

\* \* \* \* \* \* \*

Jesus asked the father, "How long has this been happening to him?" He said, "Since childhood. Often the spirit has thrown him down into the fire and into the water to destroy him. But, if You can do anything, have compassion on us and help us."

## Selah . . . Pause and Reflect

*Why do you think Jesus would ask the father about the situation with his son? When Jesus asked someone a question, He was not needing an answer. He usually was interested in their faith level. He could have been showing this frantic father that He cared, He was interested. He was building the man's faith in Him as a loving Savior Who wanted to help. He knew the man was struggling.*

*Heart Check: Interesting that the man wanted Jesus to "have compassion" on their dire situation. Jesus was Himself the very embodiment of compassion! He lived, breathed and acted with compassion in every situation. He showed us the Compassionate Heart of the Father, Who only wants our good all the time!*

\* \* \* \* \* \*

Jesus said, "IF *You can…*" which could be understood as Him saying, "Is that what you said?" He was picking up on the doubting heart of the father. So the real issue actually was not the power of Jesus, but the man's faith. Jesus said, "If you can believe, all things are possible to him who believes." The man's faith was shaken and he was aware of how imperfect it was. He was completely honest with Jesus. He answered with tears, "I believe," and then added, "Help my unbelief!"

## Selah . . . Pause and Reflect

*Jesus exposed the father's doubt when he used the word "if." That correction by Jesus was done in love and the man received it as wrapped in love. (Hebrews 12:5-6 tells us that the Lord disciplines (trains) those He loves.)*

*Jesus perceived that the father had a mixture of faith and doubt. Perhaps the man thought - "Jesus could heal, but would He do it this time?"*

*<u>Heart Check:</u> The father's open heart and his humble response to Jesus is a good example for us to follow. He could have been defensive or maybe been embarrassed to be shown up in public. He had none of that! Being offended or having pride make us react in the negative. This man responded with tears of humility, asking for help from Jesus. He was rewarded for it.*

\* \* \* \* \* \* \*

Jesus commanded the demon, saying, "Deaf and mute spirit, I command you to come out of him and never enter him again!" The demon shrieked and threw the boy into terrible seizures and finally came out of him! The boy lay very still, not moving. People thought he was dead. Jesus stooped down, gently took his hand, and raised him up to his feet. He stood there completely set free! Yay!

## Selah . . . Pause and Reflect

*When the father said, "Help my unbelief," it was a heart-felt prayer. Notice how quickly that prayer was answered! Jesus then immediately commanded the demon to leave, and it did. What a gracious God we have. As soon as doubt was dealt with and the father's faith was strong, then he received the miracle he asked for. He saw his son completely set free!*

*Jesus commanded the demon to come out of the boy and NEVER enter him again! Jesus made sure the man and his wife were comforted, knowing they would not see their son in that horrible condition ever again! How encouraging for them! God is so good! His gift to this couple was a precious, normal son to love and enjoy the rest of their lives!*

*<u>Heart Check:</u> We perceive that we have faith for a miracle and then we look at the circumstances and see they are getting worse! It's easy to let a bit of doubt come in. Let's be bold and pray the same as the father in our story, "Help my unbelief!" Our heavenly Father will grant that request for us, the same as He did for the father in our story. Faith is a gift from God. (Romans 12:3 says that God has dealt to each man a measure of faith.)*

*It is very beneficial to look through the Bible noticing the faithfulness of God. We will find that He is true to His Word. He does what He says He will do! When we are convinced of that, our faith will develop to where we can see the answer coming for difficult situations.*

\* \* \* \* \* \*

## WHO IS JESUS FOR US TODAY?

*Jesus is a FAITH BUILDER! He helps us to practice faith.*

*He loves when we are open and teachable with Him about faith.*

\* \* \* \* \* \*

## WHAT DID WE LEARN FROM THIS STORY?

*Continually cast our cares on Jesus.*

*Jesus wants to help build our faith and receive from Him.*

*Learn what the Word says about faith.*

*Put our name on God's promises.*

*Don't expect to stay in a difficult situation
forever. Believe Jesus for a miracle.*

*Jesus did a complete miracle; the demon would never return!*

# MAN BORN BLIND

## John 9:1-41

*John 9:1-2 Now as Jesus passed by, He saw a man who was blind from birth. And His disciples asked Him, saying, "Rabbi, who sinned, this man or his parents, that he was born blind?"*

Right before this story begins, the religious Jews had picked up stones to throw at Jesus! They seriously wanted Him dead. Consider the emotion you or I would have right after an incident like that. I'm sure I would be shaking on the inside. Not Jesus! He walked out of the area near the Temple and looked to the side of the road where He saw a blind beggar. His heart was touched and He wanted to help. This day was the Sabbath. The man was not allowed to beg on that day, as that would have been work. He was just sitting there, not saying a word.

## Selah . . . Pause and Reflect

*This man could hear footsteps as people passed him by, but he had no idea Who it was that had just noticed him and stopped. Most people who passed by him simply saw a poor man begging near the Temple. Jesus saw more than that. He saw a man made in God's image who had struggled his entire life, trying to make the best out of the limitation of blindness.*

*Heart Check: How do we see a person who has some kind of limitation? Are we willing to see someone with the same care and concern as Jesus? Would we be willing to stop and talk to the person, to encourage them, or pray for them? The disciples watched Jesus to learn how to help people. Later, they would be doing what He did. They were always in His School. So are we!*

\* \* \* \* \* \* \*

When the disciples saw the man, they asked Jesus, "Who sinned, this man or his parents, that he was born blind?" Most people in that day, including the disciples, had accepted the belief that disabilities were evidence of the judgment of God because of that person's sin. God was giving them an infirmity and no one must interfere with God's judgment.

## Selah . . . Pause and Reflect

*One beggar. Two ways of looking at him. Jesus saw the man's struggle to cope and was moved with compassion. The disciples saw him as the reason for a theological discussion. The disciples were the ones who were blind! They did not see the heart of this man who was born into a hopeless situation.*

*Sickness was not a part of God's original plan for mankind. It was only when sin entered with Adam and Eve that people had health issues. Sickness is a result of sin. That sin nature was passed along to all of us because we are part of the human race. At the cross, Jesus took the blame for all of the sin of the whole world. He set us free from sin's curse.*

*Sin is the "root" and sickness is sin's "fruit." Jesus dealt with both at the cross. We are forgiven and healed! (1 Peter 2:24).*

*Heart Check: The hearts of the disciples were calloused to the reality of the man's situation. Everyone they knew felt the same. It's so easy to look the other way; too many things on my plate right now, etc. We have many reasons for not being involved with hurting people, whether they are next door or in a foreign country.*

\* \* \* \* \* \* \*

Jesus saw the situation differently. "This man was born blind that the works of God might be revealed in him." Jesus also said that He must work the works (miraculous accomplishments) of the Father while He was still with them, declaring Himself to be the Light of the World.

Imagine this blind man listening to these incredible statements by Jesus. Can you see him leaning forward, trying to grasp the meaning of every word? There was something about the authority coming from this Voice, yet he could sense a gentle kindness as well. Jesus said He was the Light of the World. This man had never known "light;" he wondered what light would look like.

Jesus spat on the ground and made clay. He put the clay on the man's eyes and told him to go wash in the Pool of Siloam.

## Selah . . . Pause and Reflect

*Jesus had the biggest part to play in this miracle. He made clay and put it on the man's eyes and gave him instructions. The man also had a part to play in his own miracle. He had to believe the words of Jesus. He had to obey and walk to the Pool of Siloam where he could wash the clay off from his eyes. They both had a part to play.*

<u>Heart Check:</u> *Is it the same for us? We are given the Word of God which contain healing promises. Our part is to meditate*

*on those promises; believe they are true for today, and they are true for each of us individually. We put our name in each verse, like going to the pool and washing.*

\* \* \* \* \* \* \*

The man went and washed and came back seeing! He knew that it was a Man called Jesus who made the clay and told him to go and wash. When he came back, he looked for Jesus, but He had moved on.

## Selah . . . Pause and Reflect

*We are told that this man was blind from birth. He was not like the man who "saw men like trees walking." (There was a time in his life that he had sight and knew what a man looked like.) Our current man had no idea of what a man looked like. Imagine how amazing it would be for this blind man to live in a world of "sound" only and then be given the dimension of "sight!"*

*This would be a major upgrade in his life! Can you think of all the things he would now enjoy that he couldn't before? He could see people that he loved, God's amazing creation, and even the beautiful city of Jerusalem. Wow!*

*What about him being trained for a job to earn money instead of having to beg for it? Maybe someone would teach him the Hebrew written language so he could read the Torah on his own. He had a whole new life, full of amazing possibilities! Wow!*

*Heart Check: Do we take for granted the ability to see? What a blessing it is! Have you ever been in a place where there were no city lights anywhere nearby? The whole night sky is covered with stars, like they are right next to each other! Zillions of them! Praise God for eyes to see His awesome handiwork and to be blown away by His Majesty!*

\* \* \* \* \* \*

When people saw this "blind" man being able to see, some said, "Yes, he is the former beggar." Some weren't sure. He said, "Yes! It's me! Jesus healed me!"

## Selah . . . Pause and Reflect

*He gave his testimony to those who were curious, and they brought him to the Pharisees! (Oh No! Not them!) They had one thing to say: "This Man Jesus is not from God, because He does not keep the Sabbath."*

*The first defense the Pharisees made was to say - no miracle had occurred since it was the Sabbath and God would never violate the Law of rest by healing a person. That argument didn't work because the man in question could now see! His parents testified that he used to be blind but now he sees! The facts didn't matter, they were not about to believe that Jesus came from God.*

*Heart Check: You gotta love this dude! He had spunk! He said to the Pharisees, "Since the world began it has been unheard of that anyone opened the eyes of one who was born blind. If this Man were not from God, He could do nothing." Whoa!*

*The Pharisees answered him by saying, "You were completely born in sins, and you are teaching us?" Can you sense a bit of pride on their part? Oh ya.*

*The really sad part is that they excommunicated him. (v34). That meant he was not allowed to attend a synagogue service.*

\* \* \* \* \* \* \*

Jesus heard that the Pharisees had cast out the healed man and He went looking for him. Awww… He asked the man, "Do you believe in the Son of God?" The man said, "Who is He, Lord, that I may believe in Him. Jesus revealed that it was Himself. The man said, "Lord, I believe!" and he worshipped Him.

## Selah . . . Pause and Reflect

*When he was interrogated, this former blind man simply stuck with the truth as he knew it. He refused to bow to the intimidation of the religious crowd. (His parents weren't as bold as he was.)*

*Jesus heard about it and rewarded him with a personal revelation, a unique encounter with The Son of God. Those minutes spent with Jesus would be etched in his memory forever. Can you picture this man enthusiastically spreading the news about his healing everywhere he went? He could tell people that he now worships Jesus, Who radically changed his life!*

*Heart Check: What a precious Savior we have! He sees, He knows, He cares. He is aware of what we are going through. He opens our eyes to see truth from His Word. He guides us with His eye, (Psalm 32:8) and the eyes of the Lord are on the righteous. (Psalm 34:15).*

*We were all born spiritually in the dark. We were blind to God and His Kingdom. It wasn't until Jesus, The Light of the World, came into our heart that we could see truth and worship Him. The Father sees us, He knows us.*

*All this man physically saw was darkness until Jesus came into his life and gave him sight. Then he had an encounter with Jesus and worshipped Him.*

\* \* \* \* \* \* \*

## WHO IS JESUS FOR US TODAY?

*Jesus is the LIGHT in any dark situation.*

*He promises a new life, a new start, to everyone.*

\* \* \* \* \* \* \*

## WHAT DID WE LEARN FROM THIS STORY?

*Sin is the root. Sickness the fruit. If you are forgiven, healing is yours.*

*Jesus asked a person with an infirmity to "do something." Go, wash, then the healing will come. And it did come!*

*The Jesus Way - Light and Truth*
*The World's Way - Darkness and Lies*

*This brave man refused to heed those who advised him to renounce Jesus. Result: Persecution from the religious authorities and a visit from Jesus!*

# WOMAN WITH BENT BACK

## Luke 13:10-17

*Luke 13:10-13 Now He was teaching in one of the synagogues on the Sabbath. And behold, there was a woman who had a spirit of infirmity eighteen years, and was bent over and could in no way raise herself up. But when Jesus saw her, He called her to Him and said to her, "Woman, you are loosed from your infirmity." And He laid His hands on her, and immediately she was made straight, and glorified God.*

Jesus and the disciples were on their last trip toward Jerusalem. This was most likely the last synagogue He taught in. Being familiar with Bible stories, we all know that "Jesus/Sabbath/synagogue/healing" spells trouble already! (Read Matthew 12:1-14 for an example. It's interesting that they made such a fuss about someone getting healed that they ended up plotting to take Jesus' life, v14. Whoa, what's up with that?! They were the Law Breakers!).

## Selah . . . Pause and Reflect

*This woman did not come to Jesus. He called her to Himself! He was moved with compassion seeing her condition, all bent over, not able to straighten herself up. It's like He was thinking, "Wait a minute! This cannot go on! She has to be healed!" Can you sense the care He is expressing for her? He knew those were eighteen "very long" years! He spoke healing words to her, "Woman, you are loosed from your infirmity." Wow! Life-changing words! Her whole life changed right then! She will never forget that day! She will never forget the kindness and the authority of Jesus!*

*Heart Check: Picture yourself in her condition. Just for fun, do what I did - walk around bent completely over at the waist. I thought I would fall forward and I didn't think my neck would stretch back far enough for me to look up and see someone's face! What a way to live. (Heavy sigh.)*

*Think about how she must have felt when she heard Jesus call her to Himself? Her heart beat in anticipation; her hope soaring! Then He put an end to the horrible bondage she had endured for so long! She was awestruck at the power of His words! All the constriction of the bones in her back loosened and she was free!! Oh my goodness! What an amazing miracle! Jesus had released her forever from that crippling spirit. She effortlessly raised herself up and realized that all the pain was gone! The Bible says that she stood straight and tall and overflowed with praise to God! Picture everyone in the synagogue immediately standing up, cheering, clapping, praising God for an amazing miracle for this sweet sister they all loved!*

\* \* \* \* \* \*

The ruler of the synagogue was not happy because Jesus healed on the Sabbath. He sternly told the crowd that there were six days on which men ought to "work." Come and be healed on those days, not on the Sabbath day. (Everyone sat down. . . the joyful mood was shattered. . .)

## Selah . . . Pause and Reflect

*When Jesus healed someone on the Sabbath He was not breaking any Laws that God made, only the ones the Pharisees added. God rested on the seventh day. (Genesis 2:2-3). God intended the Sabbath to benefit man. This was a day for rest and refreshing; physically and spiritually. It allowed time to reflect on God's love, His mercy and many blessings. Man was to draw close to God on the Sabbath and to better understand His will.*

*The Pharisees and scribes added many restrictive laws that became a burden to the people. Jesus told those religious leaders that they were rejecting the commandment of God so that they could keep their own traditions. (Mark 7:9,13). Jesus taught the people that God's ways concern the heart, not what they would do by observing forms of religion devised by man.*

*Heart Check: God knows what is best for His children! No other Sabbath rules are needed! People who follow God's original plan of taking one day of the week off to rest and enjoy Him, His Word, friends, family and His creation will be refreshed.*

\* \* \* \* \* \* \*

Jesus told a story that illustrated the thinking of the Pharisees and scribes. He reminded each one of them that on the Sabbath they would loose an ox or donkey from the stall and lead it away to water it. Then He appealed to them to consider what just happened in front of them. Shouldn't this woman, a daughter of

Abraham, whom Satan has bound for eighteen years, be loosed from this bond on the Sabbath?

When He said these things, all His adversaries were put to shame. They knew that what He said was right. They would habitually take good care of their animals. Are not people of far greater value than an animal? Of course, they knew that; so they didn't have an answer that could justify them. The people in the synagogue loved hearing everything Jesus said! They couldn't wait to tell someone in their community about the healing they witnessed at synagogue when Jesus was there!

## Selah . . . Pause and Reflect

*Jesus drew their attention to the hypocrisy of watering livestock on the Sabbath and that being okay. That involved physical effort. In contrast, a compassionate ministry to the sick was forbidden on the Sabbath, even when it required no effort, only the words of Jesus.*

*Think about the ruler of the synagogue for a minute. If he listened to Jesus with an open mind, looking for truth, would he consider his own beliefs? Does he really believe in and serve a God that would allow an animal to be loosed that has only been bound for a matter of hours - and not allow the loosing of a woman bound for eighteen years? What kind of a God would that be? Was the ruler's mind so clouded by man-made laws and traditions that he could not see the reality of the situation?*

*Heart Check: Is there any danger that our minds can become clouded to reality and truth? Satan loves to work in our minds to bend us spiritually so our gaze is directed downward, only seeing our faults and failures. That will cause us to possibly back away from embracing the big plans the Lord has for our life.*

\* \* \* \* \* \*

Jesus called her a "daughter of Abraham." This must have encouraged her greatly. God promised to make a great nation through Abraham, a nation that would be a blessing to all the families of the earth. (Genesis 12:2-3). She was a descendant of Abraham, a part of God's chosen people, and was a recipient of those blessings!

## *Selah . . . Pause and Reflect*

*We are also recipients of the blessings of Abraham! Genesis 15 gives us the story of how God made a covenant with Abraham. This was a binding agreement which God Himself vowed to fulfill. Abraham's part was to believe everything God said. This covenant was ultimately fulfilled in Jesus. When we believe in Him, it is accounted unto us for righteousness, the same as it was for Abraham. (Genesis 15:6).*

*Heart Check: Have you received God's gift of righteousness? It's really awesome to know that all our sins are forgiven and God sees us "in Jesus" the Righteous One. (Colossians 1:27, Romans 4:13-25). What are you waiting for?! Invite Jesus into your heart! Decide to live for Him!*

\* \* \* \* \* \*

## WHO IS JESUS FOR US TODAY?

*Jesus is COMPASSIONATE and He sees us pain free, healthy.*

*He bid her to come take her healing, He wants us to do the same.*

*\* \* \* \* \* \* \**

## WHAT DID WE LEARN FROM THIS STORY?

*No one could help her until she met Jesus and He prayed for her. He is our hope! Don't give up, even after a long struggle.*

*Jesus had compassion on her immediately and called her to Himself! He took the initiative.*

*It is helpful to compare the beliefs we have with the clearly stated beliefs taught in the Bible.*

*A close relationship is what Jesus wants with us. Not us following a list of rigid rules.*

*Just as her friends in the congregation rejoiced at her healing, so we can rejoice when our friends are blessed by the Lord.*

*Wouldn't it be fun to meet this dear lady in heaven?*

# MAN WITH DROPSY

## Luke 14:1-6

*Luke 14:1 Now it happened, as He went into the house of one of the rulers of the Pharisees to eat bread on the Sabbath, that they watched Him closely.*

Jesus taught the people in one town after another as He traveled toward Jerusalem. (Luke 13:22). He was warned to stay away because Herod wanted to kill Him. His reply was, "It cannot be that a prophet should perish outside of Jerusalem." (Luke 13:33). Jesus knew it was God's timing for Him to soon experience the cross.

One of the rulers of the Pharisees invited Jesus to eat a Sabbath meal at his home. There would have been a number of Pharisees invited for that same dinner.

The Jewish Sabbath begins at sundown on Friday and ends at sundown on Saturday. The meal would have taken place in the afternoon on Saturday, perhaps at 2 or 3 pm.

## Selah . . . Pause and Reflect

*Onlookers may have thought this generous Pharisee was giving honor to Jesus by this invitation. Of course, everyone knew how important (and perhaps rich) the ruler was and how he would be able to provide a wonderful meal for all of his distinguished guests.*

_Heart Check:_ It may have looked like a kind gesture on the ruler's part, but he had far from kind motives! The Pharisees were bent on finding fault with Jesus so they would have a reason to put Him to death. Verse one comes right out and says, "they watched Him closely." (They were not intending to learn God's truth and take notes!) They wanted to catch Him in something they could accuse Him of, like healing on the Sabbath, which was prohibited by their Laws.

\* \* \* \* \* \* \*

And there was a certain man before Him who had dropsy. This was a swelling of the body caused by excess fluid in the tissues. The man did not look normal and it would be easy to see that he needed healing.

## Selah . . . Pause and Reflect

What is this man doing there? He was not wealthy and nor was he a Pharisee. Do you think that he, himself, may have wondered why he was there?! The Pharisees knew why he was there. He was their bait to trap Jesus! They were confident that the compassion Jesus had for this man would cause Him to heal him, Sabbath or no Sabbath. Jesus had done this time and again. Now the religious crowd watched Jesus carefully to see if He would do it again and violate the Sabbath.

_Heart Check:_ Do we have that same confidence in the compassion of Jesus to heal someone who needs healing? To heal us? Looking through the gospels, we see how many times compassion rose up in Jesus and He ministered healing. It didn't matter what time of day or night. It didn't matter if

*Jesus was hungry or tired. He loved people and He did not like to see them suffer.*

\* \* \* \* \* \* \*

Jesus knew the man with dropsy was planted there simply to trap Him. The religious crowd had already decided Jesus most likely got His miracle working power from Satan. (Mark 3:22). This meal was all about simply gathering more evidence to convict Him of crimes worthy of death.

## Selah . . . Pause and Reflect

*What we believe is so important! If the Pharisees, scribes and teachers of the Law had simply agreed with what God said when He gave The Law to Moses, they would have no reason to hound Jesus for breaking it! HE didn't break God's Law, THEY did! They added many petty rules to keep on the Sabbath. God made the Sabbath to be a day of rest, a day to enjoy the Creator and to thank Him for providing everything they needed by His grace.*

*Heart Check: Adam was created on the sixth day and God made the seventh day a time to rest. On Adam's first day, he didn't have to till the soil for a garden, plant trees or anything else! It was all provided for him by the Grace of God. He simply plucked the fruit, enjoyed it and thanked the Lord. Let's pluck the fruit! Jesus conquered the sin barrier between us and God, having become sin for us and consequently being judged guilty by God the Father.*

*God so loved us that He gave us His Son to provide salvation for us. There are no works on our part. We just take what is offered to us, which is Jesus to forgive us and come live inside of us. Just like Adam ate the fruit provided by grace, we can rest in God to provide everything we need by grace. It's ours for the taking. Pluck and eat!*

\* \* \* \* \* \*

Jesus asked the experts in the law and the Pharisees, "Is it lawful to heal on the Sabbath?" No one answered His question. So Jesus turned to the sick man and took hold of him. He then healed him and released him to go.

## Selah . . . Pause and Reflect

*Are you surprised that no one answered Jesus? I picture Jesus as having a commanding presence, an incredible confidence mixed with genuine love for all people, including the ones He was speaking to. He wanted to win their hearts. We do know that Nicodemus and Jospeh of Arimathea followed Jesus; hopefully many other Pharisees did as well.*

*Heart Check: Verse four tells us that Jesus "took hold of the man." That sounds like He embraced him. Wouldn't that be so meaningful to this man? He would never forget what he felt when the Son of God gave him a hug!*

*This man had nothing to do with his healing! We don't know if he believed in Jesus or not. He didn't ask to be healed, he was just told where to stand! He had no idea of why he was invited to a Pharisee's home for a meal. He felt completely out of place. He didn't say a word while he was there.*

*How fun it would be to see the faces of this man's family when they saw him coming home perfectly normal! I'm sure his smile went from ear to ear! He was pretty happy about being made whole! Wow, he had his life back!*

\* \* \* \* \* \* \*

Jesus asked a question to get this religious group to see how distorted their values were. He said, "If one of your children or your animals fell into a well, wouldn't you do all you could to rescue them even if it was a Sabbath day?"

## Selah . . . Pause and Reflect

*There was silence. If they told the truth, they would confess to be breaking the same Sabbath Laws that they are accusing Jesus of breaking. Jesus wanted them to see the loving heart of the Father Who gave them a day to rest. It was meant to be refreshing, not to be a frustrating day with petty rules that made life difficult.*

*Heart Check: Jesus took the seat of authority in this story. He had His way! Not the Pharisees, who wanted everyone to obey them.*

*Who has taken the seat of authority in my life or in your life? Are we doing life God's way, receiving the blessings of His grace? Or, do we strive to prove ourselves worthy? Jesus lives in us; He makes us worthy! That's grace!*

\* \* \* \* \* \* \*

*WHO IS JESUS FOR US TODAY?*

*Jesus is our GRACE GIVER! We don't earn blessings.*

*He destroyed the sin barrier between us and the Father.*

\* \* \* \* \* \*

*WHAT DID WE LEARN FROM THIS STORY?*

*This man was part of a set-up by the religious rulers to discredit Jesus. For him, it turned out to be the GRACE of GOD that gave him complete healing!*

*Jesus always gets the last word! He can make difficult circumstances into blessings for us. Only He can turn something bad into good, like He did for this man.*

*Jesus did not have a formula for how He ministered healing. Some He laid hands on a shoulder or touched skin. He put His fingers in ears of the deaf and His spit on eyes of the blind. This man He hugged. Precious.*

*Jesus told stories to reveal Pharisee pride. This must've been a difficult meal for those pious men to sit through! If they were smart, they listened!*

*Don't forget to "pluck the fruit!" Enjoy the benefits that Jesus has already paid for and will give to us freely.*

# LAZARUS COME FORTH

### John 11:1-44

*John 11:1-3 Now a certain man was sick, Lazarus of Bethany, the town of Mary and her sister Martha. It was that Mary that anointed the Lord with fragrant oil and wiped His feet with her hair, whose brother Lazarus was sick. Therefore the sisters sent to Him, saying, "Lord, behold, He whom You love is sick."*

Bethany was a small town located about two miles east of Jerusalem. Jesus enjoyed a close friendship with Lazarus and his sisters, Mary and Martha. (During the final week before the Crucifixion, Jesus spent considerable time in Bethany with His friends.)

Jesus taught the people and performed miracles in and around Jerusalem and Jericho in the area called Judea. Jesus taught that He was the Son of God. The Jews accused Jesus of blasphemy because they considered Him to simply be a man. They picked up stones to stone Him. (John 10:31-34).

Because of that confrontation, Jesus and His disciples went to the Jordan River to the place where John the Baptist had been baptizing. Many people came to see Jesus there and believed in Him. This place was about 20 miles from Bethany, a two-day walk. This is where our story begins.

## Selah . . . Pause and Reflect

*The three siblings were very familiar with how Jesus healed anyone and everyone that came to Him. They had seen it with their own eyes and also heard many stories from Jesus and the disciples as they passed through Bethany and stayed with that family. When Lazarus became seriously ill, the sisters knew they had no worries. They would simply get in touch with Jesus and He would come immediately to raise up His best friend.*

*Heart Check: Notice what the sisters said in their message to Jesus, "Lord, behold, He whom You love is sick." They were calling on the one thing they knew for sure about Jesus - He was full of compassion! They had seen it many times when Jesus healed people. The sisters eagerly watched and waited to see Jesus come, thinking "maybe today."*

\* \* \* \* \* \* \*

When Jesus received the message that His friend was sick, He said, "This sickness is not unto death, but for the glory of God, that the Son of God may be glorified through it." Then He stayed two more days in the place where He was. (He was following the directions of His Father, knowing that a greater miracle was planned. People would see that Jesus had power over death.)

## Selah . . . Pause and Reflect

*This miracle confirmed the fact that Jesus was The Resurrection and Life! The news of Jesus raising Lazarus spread rapidly, causing religious Jews to have an urgency to kill Jesus. They had to maintain control; things were getting out of hand.*

*They were losing their people to this heretic. Jesus was getting glory and they didn't like it! Jesus had to go, for the good of the people.*

*Heart Check: Jesus listened to the voice of the Father for instructions in every situation. First, let's see what Jesus did NOT listen to. 1) He did not listen to His feelings. Jesus had a strong friendship with Lazarus. This was a person He cared about very much. In the natural, He would want to bring help immediately. 2) He did not listen to His own reasoning or what He did in the past. 3) Jesus did not listen to concern regarding his safety. He stayed in supernatural rest and calm, knowing the ways of God are always right and good.*

*Jesus did not dictate to the Father when to act or how to act. He simply obeyed. The important thing for us, is to keep our relationship with the Father strong. He loves each one of us and wants the best always. He will tell us what to do and then give us the ability to do it! (Philippians 4:13). What is He saying to us?*

\* \* \* \* \* \*

When Jesus told the disciples they were heading back into Judea, they were not too excited about that! They reminded Him the Jews there were about to stone Him. "You're going there again - and taking us with You??!"

## Selah . . . Pause and Reflect

*Jesus reminded them that there are only twelve hours in a day that a man can do the Lord's work. Jesus would do the Father's will, regardless of the danger. He did not want to lose this opportunity to work while He could. He knew that soon He would be hanging on a cross and His time on earth would be finished.*

*Heart Check: Jesus made it plain to the disciples that Lazarus was not just sleeping, he had died. Jesus wanted each of them to know that His power was available to not only heal the sick, but to raise the dead.*

\* \* \* \* \* \* \*

Thomas said to his fellow disciples, "Let us also go, that we may die with Him." The courage of his statement was motivated by his love for Jesus. These twelve had three years of daily interaction with the most amazing Man that ever lived! Eleven of them were committed to Jesus, come what may. Judas will soon show himself to be a traitor.

## Selah . . . Pause and Reflect

*Daily interaction with the most amazing Man that ever lived is our recipe for success. Many things want to take us away from being alone with our Savior. He wants us to bathe in His love, guidance and encouragement.*

*Heart Check: Jesus talked about taking advantage of the time we have to do His will. He has a plan and purpose for every person! He will give us something we can do that will count for eternity; something that God has fashioned us to do. Ask the Father; He will talk to you about your purpose.*

\* \* \* \* \* \* \*

When Jesus arrived near Bethany, He learned that Lazarus had been dead for four days. Martha came out to meet Him and said, "Lord, if You had been here, my brother would not have died." Jesus said, "Your brother will rise again." She thought He meant at the Last Day Resurrection. She could not imagine or have faith for a healing miracle once death had occurred. Martha had an "if only You had come" mindset about the past, an "impossible to heal" mindset about the present, and a "wait until the end of time" mindset about a future healing.

Jesus told Martha, "I AM the Resurrection and the Life! He who believes in Me, though he may die, he shall live. And whoever lives and believes in Me shall never die." Jesus chose Martha to reveal that HE IS LORD OVER ALL, including death! Martha got it! She said to Jesus, "You are the Christ, the Son of God, Who is come into the world."

## Selah . . . Pause and Reflect

*Death is not the end. Each one of us has a soul that will live forever. Death is simply relocating! For someone who has made Jesus their Lord, death means that person is absent from the body and present with the Lord.*

<u>*Heart Check:*</u> *Jesus wants everyone to know that He has power over life and death. This life is extremely short compared to the endless centuries we will spend in the next life. It's important to know for sure if you are going to heaven and will be with Jesus, or you will be in darkness separated from Him forever. The Lord never intended for anyone to experience that hell. That's why Jesus went to the cross, to make a way for us to be in heaven forever. If you are in doubt about where you will*

spend eternity, simply surrender your life to Jesus, invite Him into your heart and make Him your Lord.

\* \* \* \* \* \*

Mary came weeping to where Jesus was and said the same words her sister said, "If You had been here, my brother would not have died." Mary was followed by many friends who came to comfort the sisters. When Jesus saw Mary weeping, His heart melted with compassion and He wept.

## Selah . . . Pause and Reflect

*For Jesus to weep demonstrates the love He has for people. He is not above all of us, He understands our grief and participates in it. He felt the sorrow of Mary and He wept with her. Jesus understands our humanity and emotions.*

*Heart Check: The sisters were both upset that Jesus missed the opportunity to heal Lazarus while he was still alive. It was all about the past. Jesus failed to show up. Now things were hopeless. They had no faith or even thoughts of a miracle happening in the present. What about us? Is it too late to expect a miracle from Jesus? Nothing is too late for The Great I AM!*

\* \* \* \* \* \*

Jesus gave orders to take away the stone that was in front of the burial cave. Martha reminded Jesus about what a decomposed body would smell like! Jesus reminded her to believe in Him and then she would see the glory of God. (John 11:39-40).

Jesus lifted up His eyes and said, "Father, I thank You that You have heard Me. And I know that You always hear Me, but because of the people who are standing by I said this, that they may believe that You sent Me." Then Jesus cried out with a loud voice, "Lazarus, come forth!"

## Selah . . . Pause and Reflect

*John writes to us in 1 John 5:14,15 - "Now this is the confidence that we have in Him, that if we ask anything according to His will, He hears us. And if we know that He hears us, whatever we ask, we know that we have the petitions that we have asked of Him."*

*The first thing we must find out is the will of God in a particular situation. If His will lines up with our prayer request, then we know that the Father will hear us. If He hears us, we know we have what we asked for. Jesus knew the Father's will in this situation was to stay where He was and then go to Bethany and raise Lazarus from the dead.*

*Heart Check: Jesus called out "Lazarus come forth," which was a command, not an invitation! Jesus is teaching us how to pray IN HIS NAME, as representatives of Him on the earth. Can we do the same things He did because He currently lives inside of us? Are we not even a little bit curious to learn WHO we have living inside of us and WHAT He wants to do through us?*

\* \* \* \* \* \*

Lazarus came hobbling out of the cave, still bound with linen grave cloths. Even his face was wrapped. Jesus said, "Loose him, and let him go."

Imagine that you were standing with that group, listening to Jesus and watching everything that happened. When Lazarus came out, how would you feel? Perhaps your heart would beat fast and your jaw would drop! Then with the unwrapping came the shouts of rejoicing and praise that went on and on! What an amazing scene to witness! Lazarus was looking good! He was smiling and when He saw Jesus, he started to laugh for joy!

Did the sisters RUN to hug their very-much-alive brother?! (By the way, he smelled really good from the spices put in the grave cloths!) Then did Lazarus run to Jesus for a long hug and tears of gratitude?

Can you picture those standing by watching, wiping tears as well? Everyone could hardly wait to tell their friends and neighbors exactly what they just saw! Of course, the One they spoke about and praised was Jesus, the One Who rules over everything, even death!

## Selah . . . Pause and Reflect

*Did the Father have this miracle be more than a healing for a reason? Did He want to encourage the disciples and followers of Jesus that the Son of God would also be resurrected in the near future? Did He want to remind them one more time that healing sick bodies and even raising the dead would be in their futures as well?*

*Heart Check:* *The disciples were devastated on Good Friday at every cruel thing that happened to Jesus. They were so despondent following His death and burial. How could evil win? They were emotionally devastated, frightened and had no hope for the future. There was no answer to the "why" question . . . until the Resurrection!*

*When they saw His resurrected body, they knew He was truly more alive than ever before! He could walk through walls!! Whoa! They were with Him off and on for forty days and then watched Him rise up through the clouds. When Pentecost came, they were filled with the Spirit and that made all the difference! They were World-Changers now! They had Jesus living on the inside of each one of them by His Spirit! So do we, by the way.*

\* \* \* \* \* \*

## WHO IS JESUS FOR US TODAY?

*Jesus is the Source and Sustainer of real LIFE!*

*He takes dead things in us that we don't like, and changes them!*

\* \* \* \* \* \*

## WHAT DID WE LEARN FROM THIS STORY?

*Jesus received glory by raising Lazarus!*
*He demonstrated to everyone He is the Life Giver.*

*We must wait on God in every situation. Get God's mind and will before doing anything else.*

*The actions of Jesus were not determined by the needs of His favorite people or the threat of His enemies.*

*Have you noticed that Jesus was never frantic or anxious about anything?! Jesus had continuous peace because He tuned in to the Father and depended on Him.*

*Take advantage of an opportunity to talk about the Lord while we can, "while it is day!"*

*Ask our Master Jesus: How can we serve You best? We want our lives to count for You.*

# TEN LEPERS

## Luke 17:11-19

*Luke 17:11-13 Now it happened as He went to Jerusalem that He passed through the midst of Samaria and Galilee. Then as He entered a certain village, there met Him ten men who were lepers, who stood afar off. And they lifted up their voices and said, "Jesus, Master, have mercy on us!"*

This was the last trip Jesus made to Jerusalem. He would not pass by this village again. The lepers saw the crowd and Jesus, and they cried out as loudly as they could, pleading for Jesus to give them mercy. These men would have been a good distance away from Jesus.

Notice that the lepers addressed Jesus as "Master." Indeed He was and is just that, THE Master over all things! Remember when Jesus calmed the storm on the lake? The disciples were so amazed that they said to one another, "Who can this be (what sort of Man is this?) that even the winds and the sea obey Him?" There's always more to learn about who Jesus is!

## Selah . . . Pause and Reflect

*Luke was the only gospel writer to record this miracle. Perhaps because he was a physician, he showed an interest in Jesus' ministry to the poor and the underprivileged.*

*There was a temptation for the religious of the day to pass judgment on others through exalting the letter of the law and being blind to its spirit. Therefore, people with serious illness, such as leprosy, were seen as being punished by God for their sins. When Jesus healed them, however, it demonstrated God's mercies for all people! The ministry of Jesus helped society see lepers and others in a more compassionate way, without judgment.*

*<u>Heart Check:</u> Is God speaking to us about not being judgmental? Is He wanting us to have the same mercy toward others that Jesus has toward us? Is He wanting us to care for the poor?*

\* \* \* \* \* \*

When Jesus saw them, He said to them, "Go, show yourselves to the priests." And so it was that as they went, they were cleansed (verse 14).

Lepers were outcasts of society and they would live together, helping each other to get by. They could have come from several different towns and villages. To get their certificate of cleansing, they would be heading for their own hometown priest. It's possible that they went their different ways.

Read Leviticus 14:1-32 for the ceremony of cleansing for a leper. It's quite involved, even to the sacrifice of a lamb, which represents Jesus. When Jesus told them to go show themselves to the priest, they knew exactly what that meant. They knew that by the time they got to where their priest was, they would not have leprosy anymore. If they did have it, they wouldn't be allowed anywhere near the priest!!! They took Jesus at His Word. They knew that they would see their priest!

## Selah . . . Pause and Reflect

*Jesus ministered healing in many ways. He touched, He rebuked fever, He spoke to disease, He commanded devils and helped their faith. He is doing NONE of that this time! He simply told them to go to be examined by their Jewish priests.*

*The really amazing thing is that these ten men did just that! No more words, no questions about "the how or when," just a simple obedience. Off they went! Wow! They knew in their hearts that whatever HE said would come to pass. No need for details. It's a done deal!*

*When they started out, they chose not to pay attention to their rotting skin, running sores and putrid smell. No doubting, nothing more needed from the Master. We have what we asked for, even though we can't see it yet.*

*Heart Check: There is a big difference between doubt and faith. Doubt says, "I can't leave until You've done something and I can see a change." Faith says, "Jesus, You are faithful to perform Your Word and You have all Power to make me clean. I'm on my way!"*

*Most healing miracles Jesus performed were instant and everyone could see a change right away, especially the person receiving the healing. This story establishes the principle of delay in the manifestation of healing. Jesus is telling us not to stop believing when the prayer ends. Believe His Word, the same as the ten lepers, and then keep believing His Word some more.*

\* \* \* \* \* \*

When one of them discovered his complete healing, he turned back to find Jesus. He shouted out praises to God, and fell down at Jesus' feet, giving Him thanks. Jesus asked, "Weren't there ten who were healed? So where are the other nine? They all refused to return and give glory to God except a foreigner from Samaria." Jesus told that man at His feet, "Arise and go. It was your faith has made you well."

## Selah . . . Pause and Reflect

*Jesus was disappointed that the nine did not return to give thanks. He didn't take away their healing, He loved them anyway. He is kind to the unthankful (Luke 6:35). The nine were "cleansed" (Luke 17:14) and the Samaritan was "made well." (Luke 17:19).*

*Heart Check: The Healer is way more important than the healing! A humble heart will automatically express thanks when receiving a blessing from God or from others.*

\* \* \* \* \* \* \*

*WHO IS JESUS FOR US TODAY?*

*Jesus is a FRIEND to all those that society rejects.*

*He hears our cries for healing and acceptance.*

\* \* \* \* \* \* \*

*WHAT DID WE LEARN FROM THIS STORY?*
*Jesus is the Master of all things!*
*Nothing is too hard for Him!*

*It's not our job to make judgments about people.*

*We can learn from the faith of the ten lepers!*
*They "went" first and then they "saw."*

*Not all healings are instant. Some are progressive.*

*Always be thankful! God will reward a grateful heart.*

# BLIND BARTIMAEUS

Matthew 20:29-34      Mark 10:46-52      Luke 18:35-43

*Luke 18:35 Then it happened, as He was coming near Jericho that a certain blind man sat by the road begging.*

Jesus was on His final journey through Jericho; on the way to Jerusalem to experience death on a cross. He was accompanied by His disciples and a large crowd of people.

We're told that Bartimaeus sat by the road begging. What would our lives be like if you and I were blind in the time of Jesus?

## Selah . . . Pause and Reflect

*The effects of blindness could be devastating, especially for those without a family to care for them. Just to exist the blind would have to depend on people for food, lodging and necessities like clothing. Most had no way to earn money, so they resorted to begging. Hopelessness would make them feel discouraged. They were ignored by society, sometimes shunned.*

*<u>Heart Check:</u> If you were blind, would you feel like an important person to the those around you? Or, would you feel like you are always bothering them to do something for you or answer your questions? Would you wonder why you were born this way?*

\* \* \* \* \* \* \*

Bartimaeus heard the noise of a crowd coming by on the road. He asked what it meant, and was told that Jesus of Nazareth was coming. When he learned that He was passing by, he cried out, saying, "Jesus, Son of David, have mercy on me!"

Those standing nearby warned him that he should be quiet; but he cried out all the more, probably even louder! "Son of David, have mercy on me!" Faith welled up inside of Bartimaeus that made him want to ask for the impossible rather than being limited by it.

## Selah . . . Pause and Reflect

*In his bold attempt to get the attention of Jesus, Bartimaeus is showing us the desperation that probably was in the heart of every blind person. Their lot in life was difficult to say the least. To live a normal life meant one had to have eyes to see.*

*His resolve to get his miracle also showed his bold faith to believe that Jesus not only could heal him, but that He would heal him! Twice he called out "Son of David," the term used for the Messiah. Bartimaeus knew when the Messiah came, He would perform many miracles, including giving sight to the blind. Now, on this day, the actual Messiah was passing by! How unexpected and amazing! Bartimaeus was beyond excited!!*

*<u>Heart Check:</u> Is it wrong to ask for good things, even miracles? Are we supposed to settle for our lot in life? Just make the best of things? If that was the thinking of Bartimaeus, he would have remained blind. What about us? Can we tap into that courage and faith that Bartimaeus had? It's really a choice to believe that God is good and He heals people today. Why not us?*

\* \* \* \* \* \* \*

Jesus had the ability to pick out a personal call for help over the din of the noisy crowd around Him. He heard the cries of Bartimaeus and He stopped.

He told those nearby to bring the man to Him. Then the same ones who told Bartimaeus to keep quiet are now telling him, "Cheer up! Get up! Jesus is calling for you!" Wow, what good news that was! He threw off his beggars' cloak; he was done with that! He jumped up and made his way to Jesus.

## Selah . . . Pause and Reflect

*It's interesting that the people who made Bartimaeus feel that he was insignificant and he must keep quiet, are the same ones who now will have to tell him that Jesus saw him as significant and is calling for him!*

*Many people were simply onlookers, walking with Jesus or standing along the street. They were not expecting Jesus to help them. And, that's what they got - nothing! Bartimaeus was expecting and he received what he wanted!*

*Heart Check: Which group are we in? Are we content to learn about Jesus, but that's as far as it goes? Can we muster up the courage and faith to believe Jesus' own words: "Ask and it shall be given to you?" (Luke 11:9). Let's be like Bartimaeus and ask for the impossible rather than being limited by it!*

*Can we thank Jesus for the answer, even before it comes? Bartimaeus must have had so much Joy and a Thankful Heart when he tossed off his beggar's cloak! He knew he was heading for a life of seeing things with his own eyes!*

\* \* \* \* \* \* \*

Jesus asked, "What do you want Me to do for you?" Bartimaeus answered with humility and respect. "Rabboni, (Master), that I may receive my sight."

## *Selah . . . Pause and Reflect*

*It seems odd that a blind man would be asked by Jesus - "what do you want?" It's like, we all know what he wants - his sight!! Right?! Jesus wanted him to make a specific request, not something general. He wants the same from us. Faith works best on specifics because then we will know exactly when the answer comes.*

*Perhaps Bartimaeus heard stories of Jesus healing blind people. News travels fast! People talk! There were the two blind men at Capernaum and one at Bethsaida. Those stories, and others, made him confident, knowing it was the will of God to open blind eyes. "…If we ask anything according to His will, He hears us. And if we know that He hears us, whatever we ask, we know that we have the petitions that we have asked of Him." (1 John 5:14-15). Bartimaeus went from hope to faith when He knew God's will.*

*Heart Check: Does our healing depend on how much we do to deserve a touch from God? No, our healing depends on what Jesus did for us! He took stripes and He did that because of His awesome love for each one of us. Can we ever deserve to be healed? Is our healing based on our performance? No.*

\* \* \* \* \* \* \*

Jesus responded to Bartimaeus with compassion, "Go your way; your faith has made you well." Immediately he received his sight and followed Jesus on the road.

## *Selah . . . Pause and Reflect*

*In Matthew and Mark, the story of Bartimaeus is directly preceded by another instance where Jesus was asked to do something. Jesus said to James and John, "What do you want Me to do for you?" (The same question He asked Bartimaeus.) Those two brothers wanted to sit on the right and left of Jesus in His glory. Their motivation was to be exalted with Jesus.*

*We know the motivation of Bartimaeus because of what he did directly after he was healed. You would think that he would hurry to find people that he knew, all while taking a long look at his town and surroundings. He didn't do any of that. He wanted to follow Jesus and be close to Him. He walked down the road with Him. The motivation Bartimaeus had for eyesight was very different than James and John. (We do know from Scripture that in time, James and John both became totally surrendered to live for Jesus only and not for any glory of their own.)*

*Heart Check: What are our priorities? What is our motivation? Is Jesus Number One? We can tell by how we spend our time. We will always find time and a way to do what we really want. Let's follow Jesus and walk down our road with Him!*

\* \* \* \* \* \* \*

## *WHO IS JESUS FOR US TODAY?*

*Jesus is THE ANSWER to the cries of desperate people!*

*He loves our passion about dreams, visions, destiny.*

*\* \* \* \* \* \* \**

## *WHAT DID WE LEARN FROM THIS STORY?*

*Jesus is always passing by our road, always available for us to call out to Him.*

*Jesus hears the cry of every passionate seeker.*

*Know that God's will is always to heal everyone. Jesus proved that by healing blind Bartimaeus.*

*Don't be influenced by those who don't see us as significant. Jesus does!*

*Do we have something that disturbs us so much that it makes us to be a disturbance?*

*Do we ever deserve to be healed? No. Is our healing based on our performance? No. Our healing is given to us freely and is based on the stripes Jesus took and the blood that He shed for us.*

*Our priority in life is the same at Bartimaeus - to stay close to Jesus; to hear and obey Him.*

# HEALING OF MALCHUS' EAR

Matthew 26:36-51          Mark 14:43-50

Luke 22:47-51          John 18:1-11

*Matthew 26:47-49 …Judas, one of the twelve, came with a great multitude of Roman soldiers with swords and clubs.They took orders from the chief priests and elders of the people. Now Judas had given them a sign, saying, "Whomever I kiss, He is the One; seize Him." Immediately he went up to Jesus and said, "Greetings, Rabbi!" and kissed Him.*

Jesus and His disciples celebrated the Passover meal together in the upper room. Many hundreds of Passover Lambs shed their blood that day. Jesus knew His time had come to become the Lamb of God sacrificed for all humanity.

After eating the Last Supper, Jesus and the eleven went to a favorite spot on the Mount of Olives, a garden called Gethsemane. Jesus separated Himself and prayed earnestly, saying, "Not my will, but Yours be done."

Because He was familiar with Psalm 22, Jesus knew the horrors that lay ahead for Him during those many agonizing hours ahead. He also knew how God would exalt Him in glory after His resurrection. It was love for all of us that kept Him steady on course to accomplish a great deliverance for all mankind. He would have a forever family, free from the shackles of sin.

As soon as Jesus finished praying, Judas, the betrayer, came to the garden. He led a large company of well-armed soldiers, sent by the chief priests, scribes and elders.

## Selah . . . Pause and Reflect

*Judas kissed Jesus on the cheek like someone would warmly greet a very close friend. Jesus remarked, "You're betraying Me with a kiss?! Really?" Judas didn't answer or say anything more. Jesus took over the conversation from then on.*

*Heart Check: Jesus was in charge of the entire arrest scene from the very beginning! He laid down His own life, no one took it from Him.*

\* \* \* \* \* \* \*

Jesus stepped forward and asked them, "Whom are you seeking?" They said, "Jesus of Nazareth." Jesus answered and said, "I AM." As soon as He said that, they all fell backwards to the ground! They didn't see that coming! How humiliating! Those trained soldiers must've felt kinda sheepish as they scrambled up!

The chief priests, elders and Pharisees were very familiar with the God Who gave His Name to Moses as "I AM." (Exodus 3:14). The experts in the Law that were present must have been surprised and profoundly impacted by that demonstration of power. Most likely, they were enraged at hearing a "mere man" use the term "I AM," claiming Himself to be the Almighty!

The religious leaders had long since decided that Jesus did not represent God because He did not keep the Sabbath like they did.

They felt they were honoring God by getting rid of this imposter who influenced so many.

As they were picking themselves up, they must have reasoned that Jesus was being used by Satan to have such powers. Already they suspected that Jesus did miracles by the power of Beelzebub, who represented Satan. (Matthew 12:24).

## Selah . . . Pause and Reflect

*We're told in Luke 22:2-5, that the chief priests and the scribes sought how they might kill Jesus. Then <u>Satan entered Judas</u>, surnamed Iscariot, who was numbered among the twelve. So he went his way and conferred with the chief priests and captains, how he might betray Jesus to them. And they were glad, and agreed to give him money.*

*Satan <u>was</u> on the scene that night. He was not in Jesus, he was in Judas!*

*<u>Heart Check:</u> When every man was helplessly flattened, it was quite plain to all that Jesus was totally in charge! All of the trained soldiers had lethal weapons. Yet, they fell backwards while facing an unarmed man! What impact do you think that had on the hearts and minds of those soldiers? They knew that the only way they could arrest Jesus was if He allowed it.*

*What weapon did Jesus have? His weapon was the Living Word of God coming out of His mouth. We have the same weapon as well. The Word of God is powerful when it is comes out of our mouth! (Hebrews 4:12).*

*Jesus laid down His life because of His great love for all of us. He humbly accepted the plan and will of the Father.*

\* \* \* \* \* \*

Jesus asked them again, "Whom do you seek?" They said, Jesus of Nazareth.

He responded again that He was that Person. He then said, "Since I'm the One you seek, let all of these with Me go their way." He spoke to His Father: "Those whom You gave Me I have kept; and none of them is lost except the son of perdition, that the Scripture might be fulfilled." (John 17:12).

## Selah . . . Pause and Reflect

*Typical of our Savior, Jesus was mindful of protecting the eleven that He loved so dearly. In every healing miracle we have looked at, we've seen Jesus be full of care and compassion for the one in front of Him.*

*Heart Check: Do we fully comprehend how much care and compassion Jesus has for each one of us? Think about it. No one is left out. Picture yourself as the one in front of Him right now. He knows you and He loves you.*

\* \* \* \* \* \*

It was at this time that, in the eyes of the disciples, everything was going south. Why would Jesus say - let these go their way? Why would the servant of the High Priest come forth to arrest Jesus? What is going on?! A soldier with ropes stepped forward. This is not happening!

Simon Peter, having a sword, drew it and struck the high priest's servant, cutting off his right ear. The servant's name was Malchus. Jesus said to Peter, "Put your sword into the sheath. Shall I not drink the cup which My Father has given Me?" Those were hard words for Peter to hear.

## Selah . . . Pause and Reflect

*Standing in front of Peter there were hundreds of trained soldiers, armed with clubs and spears. Obviously, Peter acted impulsively, he wasn't thinking, he was reacting from his heart. Peter was a fisherman, not trained to wield a spear! It was a good thing that it was only an ear that was severed. Peter would spend the rest of his life in prison, or be executed by the authorities if he had taken a life in his zeal to protect Jesus.*

*Peter had a plan for Jesus which did not include His arrest and possible death! Peter forgot about his previous rebuke to Jesus and the reaction he got from Jesus: "Get behind me, Satan! You are an offense to Me, for you are not mindful of the things of God, but the things of men." (Matthew 16:23). Peter loved Jesus so much, he simply could not accept that Jesus would be killed and raised the third day. (Matthew 16:21-22). Peter thought his plan was better than God's plan. Do we ever think that way?*

*<u>Heart Check:</u> It's true that Jesus rescued His star disciple, the one He had trained for leadership the past three years. However, Jesus was focussed on more than just keeping Peter from being arrested. The "more than" was when Jesus touched and healed His enemy. Jesus came to earth to reveal the heart*

*of the Father. Jesus showed us the unconditional love of God for all, friend and foe alike.*

\* \* \* \* \* \* \*

Let's look at this man, Malchus. It is interesting that the Bible tells us the name of the High Priest's servant. Usually, a servant is not named. The name Malchus means "king." We see a King healing a king. Hebrews 2:17 tells us that Jesus Himself is our merciful and faithful High Priest.

Being a Jewish boy, raised in Hebrew school, Malchus would have known that the Name - I AM - could only apply to Jehovah God Himself. When Jesus spoke those two words and everyone (including Malchus) fell backwards, Malchus must have had an "Ah-ha" moment. Can you picture Malchus approaching Jesus in a bit of fear and trembling, knowing that Jesus was the Greater and he was by far the lesser. His eyes wide open, his hands a bit shaky, he arrested Jesus, as he was commanded to do.

## Selah . . . Pause and Reflect

*Malchus had bright red blood on his skin! And, he had a perfectly normal ear, attached with no stitch marks! Malchus was a walking visual of the mercies of God. His healing would show what a good, good God we have! Malchus had quite a story to tell his wife when he got home that night! One look at him and she couldn't wait to hear what happened!*

*Heart Check: God demonstrated His own love toward us, in that while we were still sinners, Christ died for us. (Romans 5:8). Jesus did not hesitate to heal Malchus because He knew salvation and healing were His Father's will, freely given and available for anyone. That's what the cross provides for us!*

\* \* \* \* \* \* \*

## WHO IS JESUS FOR US TODAY?

*Jesus is MAJESTY, PURE LOVE, HUMILITY and AMAZING COURAGE.*

*He willingly went to the cross for us. There is no one like Jesus!*

\* \* \* \* \* \* \*

## WHAT DID WE LEARN FROM THIS STORY?

*Jesus knew of the horrors He was about to face. In the garden He prayed, "Not My will, but Yours be done."*

*Jesus is the Great I AM, King of Kings, Lord of Lords!*

*Jesus was totally in charge during the arrest scene!*

*Peter made a mistake, a pretty big one. Jesus turned it around for good. He will do that for us too!*

*Jesus is full of care and compassion for all of us, even our enemies. Love is powerful.*

*Will Malchus be in heaven? No doubt Jesus touched his heart as well as his ear!*

*Lord Jesus, give us a New Ear to hear You better!*

Printed in the United States
by Baker & Taylor Publisher Services